Dark Psycho Manipulation

Improve Your Life, Defending Yourself from Dark Psychology. The Practical Guide to How to Recognize Deception Techniques, Mind Control, and Body Language

Chris Wheatley

© **Copyright 2020 – All rights reserved.**

ISBN : 9798695980233

The content contained within this book may not be reproduced, duplicated or transmitted without direct written permission from the author or the publisher.

Under no circumstances will any blame or legal responsibility be held against the publisher, or author, for any damages, reparation, or monetary loss due to the information contained within this book, either directly or indirectly.

Legal Notice:
This book is copyright protected. It is only for personal use. You cannot amend, distribute, sell, use, quote or paraphrase any part, or the content within this book, without the consent of the author or publisher.

Disclaimer Notice:
Please note the information contained within this document is for educational and entertainment purposes only. All effort has been executed to present accurate, up to date, reliable, complete information. No warranties of any kind are declared or implied. Readers acknowledge that the author is not engaged in the rendering of legal, financial, medical or professional advice. The content within this book has been derived from various sources. Please consult a licensed professional before attempting any techniques outlined in this book.

By reading this document, the reader agrees that under no circumstances is the author responsible for any losses, direct or indirect, that are incurred as a result of the use of the information contained within this document, including, but not limited to, errors, omissions, or inaccuracies.

Congratulations on purchasing

Dark Psychology and Manipulation
And thank you for doing so.

With your purchase, in addition to the book, you have access to the

"*10 Simple Tips to Avoid Manipulative People*" completely free!!

Go to this link below to access it!!

https://forms.aweber.com/form/25/1703173525.htm

TABLE OF CONTENTS

Introduction 5
Chapter 1: Deception Techniques 10
   Common Traits of Deception 11
Chapter 2: Emotional Manipulation 24
   The Signs to Look For 25
   How to Avoid It 33
Chapter 3: Body Language 41
Chapter 4: Dark Neuro-Linguistic Programming 55
   How to Protect Yourself 57
Chapter 5: Brainwashing 71
   How to Avoid It 75
Chapter 6: Mind Control 85
Chapter 7: Toxic/Harmful Relationships 98
Chapter 8: The Three Personalities 113
   Narcissist 114
   Machiavellian 118
   Psychopath 123
Conclusion 128
References 130

Introduction

You are familiar with the study of psychology and its relation to human emotions by way of the mind and behavior. Still, there's another branch of psychology that is less familiar to most people—dark psychology. Defined as the study of the human condition and the need to prey upon the weak, it is a fascinating topic that can explain a lot about the people in your life. Those who use dark psychology to their advantage are usually motivated by something deviant and/or criminal. Many abusers use dark psychology to get what they want from others, and they are not concerned about hurting feelings or taking advantage of people. These instinctual urges are no coincidence; however, dark psychology derives from a place of deep emotional upset.

Most of us have slight dark psychological tendencies, but we never act on them. When someone cuts you off in traffic, you might have thought to rear-end them as retaliation because you are so angry. The rational side of you kicks in, telling you that it is not worth it and that it would harm you in the process. Some people cannot control these impulses. Dark psychology will not always manifest in physical ways, but it can. More often, it is going to appear as manipulation tactics or emotionally abusive behavior. Someone who acts on these impulses loves being in control. They will stop at nothing to get what they want, even if that means hurting someone they care about.

It is thought that each one of us has this dark potential lurking below the surface. For the most part, we can control these tendencies and replace them with healthy coping behaviors. That isn't true for everybody, though. You will encounter an abuser or two in your lifetime, and it is vital to know how to deal with this when it happens. If you are not careful, you can easily get caught up in their deception, suffering at their hands. This book is meant to guide you away from those who give in to these dark psychological tendencies. When you are able to protect yourself from this kind of energy, it feels empowering.

Knowing that you do not have to put up with it is the first step toward breaking free—you do not deserve to be treated poorly, even if you feel you have made some mistakes along the way. You are only human, and your mistakes will teach you lessons. If you have someone in your life who mistreats you, now is the time to stand up for yourself finally. Carefully and deliberately, you will learn methods and techniques that are psychologically proven to work on abusers and others who cannot control their impulses. When you realize you are not helpless, this is going to give you a lot of strength.

The concept of dark psychology isn't new. It is thought to be a universal condition that anyone can experience; some are more predisposed to the trait than others. This factor drives most people who have the ability to hurt, maim, steal, or even kill. Throughout history, this has been happening for several hundreds of years. In your average lifetime, you are probably not going to encounter a serial killer or serial robber. Still, youdefinitely might mistakenly open yourself up to someone who has bad intentions with your feelings and emotions. Unfortunately, it is in human nature to get ahead, and those who act on these impulses driven by dark psychology will stop at nothing.

There is a potential to misinterpret dark psychology with aberrant psychology, but the two are different. As described, uncontrollable urges and impulses drive dark psychology. There is typically the intention to harm someone or something. Aberrant psychology refers to behavior that is abnormal or irregular. A person who behaves this way might have unusual sexual preferences or high self-interest. There is not always going to be a level of danger involved as there is with dark psychological behavior.

In 2018, researchers at the University of Copenhagen released more information on dark psychology. They performed a series of studies that included 2,500 people. The researchers instructed participants to indicate how much they agreed or disagreed with the statements provided. Some examples included— "It is hard to get ahead without cutting corners" and "I know I am special because I am always told so." Through the researchers' mapping, they tested these individuals for dark psychological behaviors such as egoism, narcissism, sadism, spitefulness, and more. The one common denominator they found among people defined as "dark" was intelligence. Typically, those who engage in dark psychology are also highly intelligent.

Given this research, it is easy to see why someone who appears to have good intentions might fool you. You might even date this person for many years before you realize they have these tendencies, and that can be one of the most jarring realizations to face. The intense level of deception these people possess is why you need special skills to protect yourself from those who want to drain your energy. You do not deserve to put up with this treatment, and you no longer have to. This book will encourage you to step outside of your comfort zone and put your feelings first. You no longer have to worry about being taken advantage of because you will now have the upper-hand.

Chapter 1: Deception Techniques

The act of deceptions is when someone purposely misleads you to achieve personal gain. They might want the satisfaction of knowing they lied to you, or they might seek a more significant "reward" for their deceptive behavior. When you are in a relationship with a cheater, you are being deceived. Your partner might lie to you about working late or going on business trips. In reality, they are spending time with someone else. In this case, they would be getting the benefits of having two romantic partners at once. It is a selfish action that they know will hurt you, so they might use deception techniques to divert attention from what they are doing. Lying about where they are and making it seem like you are overbearing are two techniques that would make sense in this case. No matter what is going on, you must be aware of the deception techniques most commonly used. It is beneficial to have this knowledge to protect yourself from them.

Deception does not always have to be a big act. It can also be something small, like being lied to about an upcoming event that hasn't happened yet. If someone is intentionally deceiving you, they might suggest that you missed said event to make you feel guilty or wrong in some way. It is essential to recognize that any time someone deceives you, it isn't going to feel great when you find out. You have every right to be hurt, confused, and untrusting after this happens to you. Do not let the person make you feel like you are overreacting or crazy because your feelings matter.

As we look into the various forms of deception, take notes on how many you have personally experienced. A lot of these actions might come as a surprise to you because most people brush them off. Having trust for the people in your life is incredibly important. If they are continually deceiving you, then that level of trust cannot be maintained. You are educating yourself for the purpose of moving forward and only letting those in who are worthy of your time and energy. Boost your self-confidence by realizing you can make this choice.

Common Traits of Deception

Deception is intentional when the person performing the action knows that it will hinder or hurt you somehow. The thing about liars is that they often know exactly what to say to make it seem like their actions are not as malicious or harmful as intended. You need to focus on the bigger picture and keep in mind that this person had prior knowledge of your feelings and how you would react. The way they act is not always going to be excusable, so do not feel pressured just to accept their behavior and move on—this only enables more deception in the future.

Lying

The most common deception technique of all, many of us lie. What makes it deceiving? Telling a lie has a specific set of boundaries attached that is not always clear. You have lied to people before, but that does not necessarily make you a deceptive person. What matters most is the intention behind the lie. In an ideal world, nobody should lie, but that isn't realistic. You have probably lied to a friend about a new haircut, telling them that you like it when you thought it didn't suit their face shape. That is the kind of lie told to spare hurt feelings. Although, if they found out about the lie, it would hurt them—this is why there is a fine line.

To recognize when someone is a deceptive liar, you need to pay attention to specific traits and patterns. If someone commits to you, no matter how small, you should expect them to keep their word. For example, if your partner tells you that they will be home by a particular time, you should expect them to be home at that time. If they get held up in traffic and arrive late, this isn't necessarily a lie. You need to make sure it doesn't become a pattern, though. If they come home late because of "traffic" for the next 12 days in a row, this will sound like an excuse to cover up behavior that they are lying about.

Knowing when to intervene is crucial because you need to know when to protect yourself. The first step is to have a conversation about the issue simply. Without being accusatory, you can ask your partner about why they always seem to be late even though traffic is never reported as bad during this time. Give them the chance to explain themselves before you make any accusatory suggestions. If you are dealing with a deceptive liar, this will only cause them to become defensive and even more misleading. They are quick-thinking and will probably be able to come up with a better excuse on the spot.

Always trust your gut instinct when it comes to lying. If something doesn't add up, ask about it. Again, without being accusatory, you can ask anyone for clarification at any time. Clarification is for your peace of mind. Depending on how they react to this request, you should get a feel for their level of honesty and sincerity. Anyone who truly cares about you and has good intentions will be willing to have this conversation and will explain without resorting to more excuses. A deceptive liar might try to turn the conversation around on you. They might question why you are prying, making you feel like you are in the wrong. This technique is in the territory of gaslighting, which will be covered shortly. Recognize the way you feel after you talk to the person. If you are not provided with clarity and have more questions instead, then there is probably something deceptive occurring.

Remember that you do not have to believe everything someone tells you, but you also don't have to let the liar know this. You can listen to their stories, mentally spot the inconsistencies, and move on while deciding what you need to do next. Always put yourself first in these situations, figuring out what you must do to get away from the liar in the most safe and healthy manner possible.

The longer you "put up with" these situations, the more enabled the person will feel. By acting passive, you send them a message that says they can keep getting away with this type of behavior. Eventually, they will recognize you as a weak person, even if that isn't true. Their lies might become more extravagant and intense, testing the waters to see what you will allow. This behavior becomes significantly damaging in a romantic relationship because of the feelings involved. Being treated this way by your partner hurts for many reasons, and you should not have to sit back and allow it to happen.

Gaslighting

Gaslighting is a complex form of deception because you usually do not recognize when it is happening to you. The person who is gaslighting you can usually do this so well that it makes you question everything you thought you knew about the situation. An example is when you ask your partner why they spent $100 at a boutique. They haven't given you any gifts, and you know that this is not a place they would normally shop. Instead of providing you with an explanation, a gaslighter will make you feel bad for asking. Your partner might explain that they bought a gift for you (a lie) and that they were planning on surprising you. It won't stop there—they will then proceed to bring up the fact that they feel you are accusatory and confrontational.

Imagine going through the above situation. At the end of it, you are going to feel terrible about yourself. Not only do you believe that your partner was doing something completely innocent, but it turns out that they led you to think that they were doing it for *your* benefit. Additionally, you are now left to question your behaviors. Are you accusatory? Does this make you a bad partner? This is what a gaslighter will do to take the attention away from them and place all the blame on you. It happens so swiftly and easily that it is no wonder you probably don't realize that they are wronging you.

With gaslighting, the individual's goal is to make you feel like you must question your judgment, memory, or perception. They want you to think that you have made a mistake or misjudgment somehow. As a result of this, you are the one who has caused a negative situation to occur. By the end of the conversation, you will believe that you must change who you are or how you are behaving. This completely distracts from the fact that the other person is being deceptive toward you. They are going to get away with it again in the future by using the gaslighting technique.

It is frustrating for someone to tell you that you are wrong or made to feel bad about yourself when you know you didn't do anything. Again, it all comes down to trusting your gut instinct. If you know you haven't intentionally done anything wrong, explain to the gaslighter that you are not guilty of what they said about you. Then, you can divert the attention straight back to the original issue you brought up. Be careful when challenging them in this way. If you push too much, they might react in a way that brings out their temper, but you always have the right to defend yourself when you know you haven't done what they are accusing you of.

Most gaslighters are only going to worsen or continue to behave the same way without professional help. No matter how much sense you try to talk into them or how much you express that their behavior hurts you, this type of deception clouds their brains. All they want is personal gain, and they will stop at nothing to get this from the people around them. As a consolation, you can probably assume that they are not only doing this to you. Those who gaslight become so good at it that they do it every chance they get. This individual is likely doing the same thing to their coworkers, friends, and even strangers they encounter daily.

You will not be able to change a gaslighter, but you do not have to put up with one. You have the right just to walk away from the situation if you can do so safely. After giving them a chance to own up to their deception and they do not take it, this is the only effort you need to make before deciding to do something different that will solely benefit you. Most people feel that if they keep trying to help a gaslighter, they will eventually change them. Deception does not work this way as it is a behavior deeply rooted in dark psychology. You need to make a plan to move on and to better your life because you do not deserve this treatment. It might feel impossible, but you have the strength to leave the gaslighter in your past.

Body Language

When someone is trying to deceive you, one way to pick up on this is by observing their body language. Non-verbal communication can say a lot—often more than words or other verbal statements. As someone is talking to you, imagine that you feel they are deceiving you. What brought you to this conclusion is likely the way the person is delivering the message to you. Maybe they are shifting in their stance, or perhaps they are avoiding eye contact; both of these actions have been linked to deception before. When someone is avoiding your gaze, this usually means they are feeling guilty or intimidated. If a deceptive person refuses to make eye contact with you, they probably fear that you will be able to tell they are lying by looking into their eyes. The eyes are a very expressive part of the face.

Of course, not every instance of avoided eye contact signifies that deception is taking place, but it can become a pattern for you to recognize. In some cases, a person avoids eye contact because they feel shy or insecure. A deceptive person will be very deliberate about their aversion to eye contact. They might try to sway your opinions subliminally by making you look elsewhere. This action is a controlling move that works very well because it is so subtle. Without realizing it, you are overlooking the fact that they aren't looking into your eyes. They will give you a reason to feel that this is normal by trying to make you mimic their gaze.

When a person does not face you directly, this can also indicate that some type of deception is taking place. Having closed-off body language usually means that the other person is feeling uncomfortable in some way. Whether they are lying to you or they do not want to let you gain too much insight into their thoughts and feelings, standing off-center slightly or facing slightly away from you might mean the person is dishonest. This is another very subtle act that you probably don't notice regularly. By becoming aware of this, you might be able to spot more patterns and habits in those you interact with.

Pay attention to a person's eyebrows and mouth shape as they talk to you, as well. These are other indicators of authentic intentions. When a person is deceptive, they might unintentionally make facial expressions that you can pick up on. For example, as your partner tells you that they were out late because they had to stop at the store, you might notice their mouth moving the side as they fidget while explaining themselves. This is something that you see they do when they are feeling nervous. In an instance like this, your partner might be lying to you and worried that you will find out the real reason behind their late arrival.

Just like any other sign of deception, take everything with a grain of salt until you can prove with factual information that the person is deceiving you. If you read into all of these signs too much, you will drive yourself crazy by overthinking. These tips and common traits are all meant to help you by starting to recognize patterns. You will find that most liars have the same body language patterns, and as you observe them, this familiarity will help you in the long run. Think of these tools as traits that you can rely on when you feel unsure about someone's true intentions. While they are not official lie detector tests, they do give you the same type of insight. Another way to observe body language is by taking a look at your own. When you start feeling uncomfortable during a conversation or situation, what do you tend to do? These patterns might not be the same as those of a deceptive person, but you will definitely notice key differences in how you act. When you are uncomfortable, your body tends to mirror the feeling by changing its physical presence. Whether you need to shift from foot to foot or let your gaze wander, these are critical signs that something is off and that you are trying to cope with it.

Speech Patterns

Did you know that the tone of someone's voice has a significant indication on the meaning intended behind their words? You have probably heard several apologies in your lifetime, but you can tell the difference between the ones that were genuine and the fake ones. It all comes down to the way a person uses their speech patterns to communicate. If you notice that their pitch is wavering, this is a sign that they might be dishonest. A change in pitch, whether it is intentional or unintentional, suggests that they are not entirely comfortable with the conversation taking place. This discomfort usually happens when they feel worried that you will see their true colors or find out their true intentions. Repeating certain words or phrases is also an indication that a person might be trying to deceive you. They are probably doing this to distract you or to manipulate you. When you hear them repeating certain information, you are going to be more receptive to it. If you bring up an issue that they do not want you to focus on, they might repeat other irrelevant information as an effort to distract you from finding out the truth. This can become a very frustrating conversation because deceptive people tend to be great at steering conversations in other directions. They assume you will follow along with what they are saying because they rely on their charisma and conviction to get you to believe in it. No matter how convincing a person is, you cannot ignore their speech patterns. If you notice anything that is off or that makes you feel weird, you do not need to agree with what is being said blindly. Your gut instinct is there for a reason, so you should always consult it whenever a situation does not feel right. Make sure you consider that there are still other possibilities as opposed to what someone tells you. It is a smart way to think because it prevents you from being too oblivious to deception. If you are not necessarily predicting the worst outcome, but you are aware that it could happen to you, then you won't get as hurt as you would if you got blindsided.

Trust is very fragile, and it is easily shattered. If a person you thought you could trust betrays you, this might skew what you thought their intentions were. Pay close attention to the way they speak to you, even compare it to how they talk to other people. Doing this is an excellent way to make your observation because you get the chance to observe from an onlooker's perspective. Take a moment to see how they talk to other people and what language they use. If there is a difference in the way they make others feel as opposed to the way they make you feel, then you need to figure out why they are treating you differently.

With these explorations, you need to be careful not to get lost in them. It is easy to go overboard and convince yourself that someone is out to get you when you are only misreading their speech patterns. Take everything you observe with a grain of salt until you have some factual information to back it up. For example, if you notice your partner is using a different tone with you, and you feel they are lying to you about something, do not automatically accuse them of lying. Only when you can see a discrepancy in a pattern or something they have told you before should you bring it up. Taking this action will present them with a fact that you can see, and it will put them in a position where they have to explain themselves. With any type of deceptive person, no matter how close you are or in what capacity you know one another, it is always best to let them do the explaining. Do not try to force words out of them because they are great at twisting what you say.

Chapter 2: Emotional Manipulation

When you realize you have someone in your life who is playing mind games with you, this can be a very discouraging discovery. Nobody wants to be taken advantage of, and emotional manipulation can become very hard to break free from. You might realize what is happening, but the manipulation can happen so quickly that you don't know what to do next. If you are tired of being manipulated in this way, you don't have to put up with it any longer. By educating yourself on what to look for and how to stop it, you won't need to waste another moment of your time being held back by those who are trying to manipulate your mind. Your emotions help you express the way you feel. For anyone to tell you or suggest to you that you are wrong for what you feel, this can create several problems. For one, you are going to question everything you feel in the future. Even though your feelings are perfectly valid, a manipulator can bring you to the point where you might start to second-guess them because you don't want to upset them or make them feel a certain way. Your feelings become less of a priority, and their happiness starts to take over—it is a toxic cycle that happens in many romantic relationships, but it can also occur platonically.

The main goal of an emotional manipulator is to seek a benefit for themselves. No matter what they have to do to get there, they will stop at nothing until getting what they want. Your feelings are no longer considered once they know that you are falling victim to their manipulation. After giving up your control to them, whether you mean to do this or not, they will believe that they can start to manipulate you even more. It is a tough cycle to break, and you might even begin to think that they have the right to control you when you used to think it was wrong. Manipulators get inside your head in a way that makes you question everything you once knew to be true.

The Signs to Look For

1. **They Maintain a "Home Court" Advantage**: Being in an environment where the manipulator feels comfortable is where they will thrive. This situation puts you in a predicament when you live with this person. If you are not already in their home environment, a manipulator will encourage you to come over or to meet at a

place that they are very familiar with. This tactic gives them an automatic advantage because they feel more powerful this way. As they claim ownership of the space, this puts you in an instant space of being disadvantaged. An example of this type of advantage is when your boss asks you to meet them in their office—this is their "home court" advantage working out in their favor. Whether they are manipulative or not, they are automatically going to have the upper hand.

2. **They Get Close to You Quickly**: Manipulators purposely share a lot of personal information with you upfront. They are quick to talk openly about their struggles and insecurities. Talking about this personal material makes them seem more vulnerable than they actually are, and it gets you to trust them quickly. You will seldom meet an emotional manipulator that stays in the "getting-to-know-you" phase for too long. They might mention how they feel a strong connection with you, taking it one step further by insisting that they have never had this feeling with anyone else. Naturally, this is going to make you feel special.

3. **They Let You Speak First**: You would think that an emotional manipulator might have a lot to say, but they

typically allow you to speak first. It is all part of the manipulation act. They seem like they are genuinely interested in hearing about how you feel or how you are doing, and they are quick to encourage you to open up to them. This tactic is a way for them to gain traction over you. Because when you talk about your problems openly, they can spot your weaknesses and use them against you. It is a trust-shattering action, but unfortunately, most manipulators have a hidden agenda.

4. **They Twist Facts**: An emotional manipulator is a master of altering your reality. You can question any facts that you truly believe when an emotional manipulator wants you to believe something else. By taking a fact and twisting it slightly, they can convince you that something happened differently, even if you know for a fact that it didn't. Their argument might be so convincing that you start to question your memory. Exaggeration is another tactic they rely on to twist facts. They might do this to make themselves look more innocent, which will get you to have a soft spot for them.

5. **They Engage in Intellectual Bullying**: When someone tries to overwhelm you by speaking with many ex-

amples, statistics, and facts, this might lead to intellectual bullying. Even if the information is not correct, an emotional manipulator might lead you to believe that they know more than you, so you should just believe what they say. They like to impose their knowledge on you hoping that you will simply accept it as reality. An emotional manipulator might use phrases like, "I wouldn't expect you to understand." or "You're new, so you won't get it right away."

6. **They Engage in Bureaucratic Bullying**: Emotional manipulators are not only fixtures in your personal life; they can also be present in your professional life. They can appear as those who like to weigh you down in business with a lot of red tape, paperwork, and procedures. When someone does this to you, they are suggesting that you are beneath them in status. They want to bring all of your flaws to your attention because this distracts you from theirs. Remember, nobody is perfect, supervisors and bosses included.

7. **They Make You Feel Sorry for Speaking Up**: Voicing your concerns takes courage, and there is nothing worse than being made to feel like you are in the wrong

for expressing an opinion. It is a strategy emotional manipulators turn to when they are trying to control you and influence your decisions. They might say something like, "I don't understand why you don't trust me." If you are genuinely concerned, a person who cares about you will understand and do their best to put you at ease. An emotional manipulator is only going to care about how others perceive them, so they will rush to make themselves look better at any chance they get.

8. **They Diminish Your Problems and Exaggerate Their Own**: When you are going through something, an emotional manipulator makes you feel like you should not feel as upset, worried, or bothered about it. On the other hand, when they are going through something, this might become equivalent to the end of the world to them. They will want you to feel sorry for them, and they might even ask you to do something that will benefit them in an attempt to make them feel better. An emotional manipulator will never do as much as you are willing to do for them. Pay attention as to who is ready to drain your energy.

9. **They Act Like the Martyr**: When someone is emotionally manipulative, they want to be recognized as a

hero. They might be willing to be the first to step in when someone is in need, but they will make the person feel bad about it. After they complete the task, you likely won't hear the end about how difficult or challenging it was for them and how they did it for your benefit. They want to get you to react emotionally, and you are likely to fall for this tactic because they already did you a favor in a sense.

10. **They Are Always "Just Joking":** Emotional manipulators are great at covering up their rudeness with the idea that they are simply "joking." They are quick to tell you that they are kidding when you become upset over something they say. The problem with this is that they are always able to get away with hurting your feelings, even if they were secretly telling the truth. This puts you in a position where you feel you must take the "joke" or be a good sport about certain things that upset you.

11. **They Never Take Accountability**: When something happens that shows the emotional manipulator is in the wrong, they will never admit it. Because they never take accountability for their actions, you will find excuse after excuse pouring out of their mouth. An emotional

manipulator is quick to point the finger of blame at anyone other than themselves. If you make a mistake, however, they are going to be very capable of insisting that you are to blame. They will bring it up frequently, even after the issue is already solved. You won't hear the end of your wrongdoings.

12. **They Always Want to One-Up You**: Imagine that you are feeling thrilled because you just got a promotion. You want to tell everyone you know about this great news. When you tell someone who is an emotional manipulator, they don't respond by congratulating you like everyone else has—instead, they respond by telling you about the last time *they* got a promotion and how successful they are now. Even in moments of tragedy, an emotional manipulator is always going to have something more severe to say or something more difficult to experience. You won't be able to get a word in edgewise.

13. **They Love to Criticize You**: An emotional manipulator loves to break down your self-esteem. Even if they do not accomplish this in obvious ways, they will use subtle tactics to make you feel bad about yourself. They might question *why* you are wearing that outfit or what

you were thinking when you got that haircut. These small but impactful insults are sure to make you question the decisions that you make and the way you feel about yourself.

14. **They Use Your Insecurities Against You**: As mentioned in the beginning of this section, an emotional manipulator wants you to open up to them. They want to know all of your flaws and downfalls so they can use them against you. Once they have you in a position where they can do so, you can expect them to bring them up at any moment they can. An emotional manipulator might even try to bring them up in front of others to embarrass you.

15. **They Give You the Silent Treatment**: Silence can feel deadly when it comes from an emotional manipulator. When they do not answer you or respond to you, this makes you feel insecure about yourself. Emotional manipulators can be very hard to read. You might be freaked out when you have no indication of what they are thinking or feeling because they refuse to talk to you. They use this technique to make you worry because they know what they are doing.

How to Avoid It

Learning about all of the ways you can be emotionally manipulated can be scary and challenging to comprehend. The good news is that you no longer have to put up with these traits in others. You can protect yourself and to step away from those who try to control you. As long as you can do so safely, these tips on avoiding emotional manipulation will help you for the rest of your life. They apply to situations you are currently in and future situations that try to develop. By having an understanding of the way an emotional manipulator thinks, you now have what it takes to outsmart them.

- **Ditch the Honesty**: You are not necessarily encouraged to lie to an emotional manipulator but know that your honesty is not going to make a big difference to them. Just because you have honesty and integrity does not mean that it will be contagious. In most cases, honesty is the best policy, but you will have to think of a different one while dealing with an emotional manipulator.

    Do not be fooled by their interest in your honest statements about the way you feel. The more you reveal to them, the more information you are giving them to use against you. If you need to vent about the situation, you might want to do so with a person you know well and trust. Only communicate necessary information with an emotional manipulator.

- **Don't Be Fooled**: There are many ways that an emotional manipulator can mislead you, but this does not mean you are inevitably going to fall victim to their traps. If you ask a manipulator to do something for you, they will likely appear as a happy volunteer. They want you to believe that they are helpful and willing to do anything for you, so when the time comes, you will be ready to do anything for them. Of course, this isn't true—they are only using you.

If they try to make you feel bad about not wanting to do them a favor, remember that you do not owe them anything. Tell that person outright when you do not or cannot complete a task that would inconvenience you. By standing up for yourself, you show that you are not merely a puppet for them to control. They might appear angry or bitter toward your response, but it is not your responsibility to deal with their emotions.

- **Know You Aren't Crazy**: Depending on how long you have been emotionally manipulated, it is common to think that there are specific ways that you think which are simply *crazy*. That is exactly what your manipulator wants you to think. They want you to believe that the way you are thinking and feeling is outlandish in an effort to control you. When you feel this way, it becomes easier for them to develop their own opinions and thoughts. They will try to impose these on you.

  If you genuinely feel something, only you know what you are feeling. These are your internal thoughts, and no emotional manipulator has access to them. Never forget the power you hold in your mindset and your way of thinking. When someone responds to you in a way that makes you seem like you are acting out of pocket, look inward. Ask yourself if you truly believe you have done anything wrong. As long as you are not intentionally hurting anyone, it is safe to say that your actions and feelings are 100% valid.

- **Don't Feel Guilty**: An emotional manipulator is great at pulling on your heartstrings. They aim to make you feel guilty for everything in an attempt to get what they want from you. When you feel guilty, they can better control you. They will use these things to their advantage, bringing them up, even when they are not relevant. For example, you might have had to miss a friend's birthday party because you were working late. The emotional manipulator might ask you to do an inconvenient favor, only to bring up the fact that you haven't been there for your friends in the past. This reminder of something you went through before might be enough to convince you to inconvenience yourself on their behalf.

Much like your innermost feelings, only you get to decide what you feel guilty about. When someone tries to guilt-trip you, they are almost always attempting to distract from their behavior. They likely feel guilty about something they have done or are trying to do so that they will switch the focus onto you. Emotional manipulators are great at changing subjects in this way.

- **Don't Stoop to Their Level**: An emotional manipulator will fight dirty. If you ever get into an argument or disagreement with one, they will be quick to bring up personal issues or sensitive topics that they know will hurt you. When you fight back in this way, this is only going to agitate the situation. The manipulator will probably become even more hurtful toward you, and nothing gets resolved. The key to getting out of these situations is to rise above them. The manipulator wants your reaction; when you don't give it to them, this drives them crazy.

Don't forget that since they are emotionally manipulating you, they are probably manipulating others in your life. They might be spreading incorrect information about you behind your back, yet they appear friendly and kind to your face. You cannot trust them, no matter how much they make it seem like they have changed their ways. An emotional manipulator will never change overnight. They must address deep-rooted psychological issues first.

- **Your Life is Worse with Them in It**: No matter how much you believe you can tolerate, keeping an emotional manipulator in your life is only going to cause continual strain. Cutting toxic people out of your life is incredibly difficult, and this is especially true when it is someone you know very well and maybe even love. You need to do what is best for you, though. If this person is intentionally hurting you, then they do not care about you on the same level you care about them. It is a hard realization to face, but it becomes necessary to use this as motivation to clear the toxicity from your life.

If you can't completely cut them out, do your best to remain at a distance. Only interact with these people when it is necessary. If you are in a relationship with them, then you need to end things in a way that is definite and clear. You do not deserve to suffer for another day, so you should stand up for yourself now before things become worse as they continue to escalate. Nothing you do is going to change an emotional manipulator. No amount of good influences in their life will be strong enough to change the way their brain works entirely. This change requires professional help.

- **You Are Not Off; It Is the Mood**: An emotional manipulator is powerful enough to change the entire mood in a group. If you realize that people you are ordinarily harmonious with now seem tense or anxious, take a look at the bigger picture. There might be someone involved who is spreading toxic energy by way of emotional manipulation. You might all be feeling it and impacted in your own way. Sometimes, it can be hard to speak up about it. This is why talking to those you trust is so important. You can create a sense of solidarity when you band together.

An emotional manipulator is always going to have problems that they want others to fix. The longer you give in to this, the more codependent you will become with that toxic person. Stand up against this by setting boundaries. If you do not want to help them, you are not obligated to do so. Put yourself as a priority, and cherish those in your life who treat you right. Any relationship requires a mutual exchange of love and care, and this goes for both romantic and platonic situations.

- **Only Take Accountability for Your Actions**: Since an emotional manipulator has no sense of personal accountability, they will pawn the results of their actions off to other people. When they mess something up, they will be the first to bring others into the mix, insisting that it was a collective effort that led to the mistake or unfortunate result. Separate yourself from their actions. You know what you did and what you did not do—avoid letting them rope you into their antics because they are only going to attempt to make you feel bad about yourself.

When you leave an emotional manipulator alone with their thoughts, this is very difficult for them. They don't want to face what they have done because they know deep down that there is something wrong. While this is a hard realization to face, it should not be done at your expense. You are not an emotional manipulator, so you should not be made to face their actions. Only say you are sorry when you know you have done something to hurt someone. Stand up for what you believe in, unphased by those around you.

Chapter 3: Body Language

We have discussed some basics of body language and how this non-verbal communication trait speaks volumes. Now, we are going to further explore the ways in which a person's body language can give away a lot about what they are feeling and thinking. In general, it is important to be aware of a person's body language. Even when you are not actively engaged in a conversation, the way they are standing and what they are doing with their hands can tell you a lot. By having a good understanding of what specific body language cues mean, you will be able to use this knowledge to protect yourself against emotional manipulation.

Imagine that you have been spending a lot of time with your partner. The two of you have been going out on the town together for several nights in a row, all of which have been very fun for you. It appears that your partner is having fun too. One day, you notice you are standing in line to purchase movie tickets, and their arms are folded with a furrowed brow. When you ask what is wrong, they say that nothing is wrong and make you feel out of line for even asking. Throughout the day, they continue to sigh and stare off into the distance—it is evident that something is wrong, even though they never admitted this to you.

The way you gathered this is by paying attention to your partner's body language. Everything from the way they were carrying themselves to the non-verbal expressions they were making led you to believe that something was not okay. This is a pattern you picked up on because you knew they were having fun in the days prior. Later on in the evening, they admit to you that they were in a bad mood all day because they got an email from their boss saying that they had to come in early every day this week. Based on your original instincts, you picked up on this even though you did not know exactly what was wrong. Even when your partner did not communicate this with you verbally, they were still sending you the message loud and clear.

When reading someone's body language, it won't always be this obvious, but these are some examples of what you can look for. If you know this person, you should be able to have a sense of what their typical attitude is and notice anything different. Even when you are talking to a stranger, you are still able to sense hostility based on body language alone. It is a great skill to have, and it will definitely protect you in the long run. When someone does not admit that they are mad at you, yet they continue to punish you, this is emotional manipulation. You do not need to put up with this, nor do you need to be left in the dark about what is going on.

Defensiveness

When you are having any conversation with anybody, one of the easiest things to do is to pick up on the tone of the conversation. You can generally tell when someone is being defensive versus when they are taking a more relaxed approach. A tell-tale sign that someone is withholding their feelings from you is defensiveness, yet you are not having an argument or a tense conversation. This action shows that they are struggling emotionally for one reason or another. Defensiveness does not only come in a person's tone of voice; it can also appear how they position their body. If you see someone in front of you with their arms folded and maintaining a stern tone of voice, it is rightful to assume there is something wrong. Even if you haven't done anything, it seems clear that something is bothering this person. It becomes frustrating when they will not admit to this, yet they continue to take their frustration out on you. Frequently shifting eye contact can be another sign of defensiveness. If the person you are talking to has trouble looking you in the eyes, this can say a lot without any words. They probably feel uncomfortable for some reason, and guilt might have something to do with this. When an emotional manipulator does not look you in the eyes, it is usually because they are lying to you or they feel guilty about using you. Of course, they would never admit this to you because this would break the personality traits that they have already presented to you. They are all about the upkeep of their appearance when it comes to other people, never wanting others to perceive them in a negative light.

When you find out precisely who the emotional manipulator is and what their intentions are, they might end up dropping the front. They like to lead you to believe that they can do no wrong, but as soon as you see the authentic version of who they are, they won't feel like they need to keep up with appearances any longer. At this point, you might notice a lot of defensive body language coming to the surface. Not only will they refuse to look at you or fold their arms as you speak, but they might even scoff after you make a statement or shake their head after you express your feelings. Anything that might make you feel bad about yourself, they will be willing to explore.

To an emotional manipulator, it is a scary feeling to be equal or inferior to someone else. They have to be superior in every situation to feel secure in who they are. Emotional manipulation is deeply rooted in insecurity and those who try to hurt you are probably hurting a lot deep down. This possibility does not mean it is okay for them to lash out at you, so it is important to stand your ground. When you notice they are acting defensive, you can take this as a hint that you do not need to reveal any more personal information to them or critique what they are doing—neither will make a real impact on them. Instead, try to stick with only what must be said until the conversation is over.

Just because they are acting defensive does not mean you need to follow suit. Stay true to how you feel, and try not to let their bad mood take over your own. Dealing with an emotional manipulator can be so hard because we tend to mirror energy. If someone is giving you bad energy, you will walk away from the conversation feeling bad, too. This phenomenon is why you must work on protecting yourself and limiting the energy you give to people who intend to misuse it. When you restrict this, you are automatically taking back some of your power. They cannot force you to give them all of the great energy you have; spend it on people who are willing to do the same for you.

Stance

Observing a stance is a fairly easy way to gauge someone's

body language. If they are standing with their whole body facing you without covering up with their arms or other distractions, this is usually an indication that the person feels comfortable and is being honest with you. Having a direct and open stance is a sign that they have nothing to hide. Of course, some of the best manipulators are great at mimicking this body language, so you cannot assume anything for sure. It should provide you with some reassurance, however, when you have a conversation with someone who acts this way. Many things can change your stance while you are having a conversation. Personal insecurities can get in the way of how you are standing, causing you to face slightly away from the person in front of you. Also, covering your body with your arms is a way to make yourself appear small, which might be how you feel if you are suffering from some type of insecurity. You will seldom see a manipulator stand this way because they want to be as intimidating as possible. If anything, they are going to make themselves appear larger. On this topic, if you have ever felt the need to take a few steps back from someone while you are having a conversation, this might be because they are intruding on your personal space. Some people don't have this awareness, but most do this intentionally. A person with bad intentions wants to intimidate you—they want you to know that they hold power in the conversation, and they will show you by encroaching on your personal space. They might also try to stand taller to appear superior.

Shuffling is another sign to pay attention to. It can either indicate that the person is feeling uncomfortable or trying to distract you from a larger truth. When you are having a conversation, and the other person just cannot seem to stand still, you will take notice of this. In many ways, this can work out to a manipulator's advantage because you are going to remember this aspect of the conversation the most. They might use other manipulation tactics to deceive you while doing this, but what you saw visually is more likely to stay in your mind.

By nature, you are probably going to mirror the stance that the other person is giving you. If they are standing directly in front of you, you will be more likely to do the same. However, if they are shuffling and moving around, you will probably feel more comfortable facing slightly away from them. Become aware of this because this can serve as a good indication of the stance they are presenting to you. If it isn't automatically apparent when you look at them, taking a look at your actions can give you some insight.

To better stand your ground, it helps to know what your base stance is. Your base stance will send the other person the message that you feel confident yet willing to listen to what they have to say. This is important when dealing with a potential manipulator because you shouldn't automatically try to shut them down—this will only anger them and cause them to lash out. Remain open-minded without fully subscribing to what they are saying to you. Stand with your arms relaxed at your side, your body facing directly in front of them.

While this base stance won't protect you from their lies, it will give you a necessary boost in confidence that they might be trying to take away from you. It is astounding how well they are able to control you without you even realizing it. When you become more aware of different stances and what they mean, you will have an upper-hand as you deal with all of the people you encounter.

Negative Speech

One thing you'll notice about a manipulator is how willing they are to talk negatively. The topic can be other people, situations, you, or even them. No matter what it is, they should have no problem expressing their negative opinions in the hopes that you will agree with them. By nature, manipulators are very negative people. They aren't going to be looking at the uplifting factors because they enjoy when things do not go as planned. This kind of pull toward chaos and disorder is what they thrive on, especially when they can enhance it.

Pay close attention to those who are not happy for you when you achieve a goal or accomplishment. A manipulator might not show outright disappointment when you succeed, but they might offer you a backhanded compliment as a response. Instead of genuinely expressing that they are happy for you or proud of you, they might say something like, "That was surprisingly good for your skill level." The language here is masked as positive, but the underlying message is still negative. Be aware that many manipulators are going to speak to you this way.

They might fool you at first, but this is a prime example of why you cannot only rely on the spoken words. You must observe all types of negativity. Of course, these instances are verbal and might be easier to spot. Negativity can also come in the form of scoffing, grunting, or facial expressions. If someone is telling you something that should be positive, but you sense that they still have a negative attitude, there might be a different underlying message. to make you feel bad about yourself, but they want you to believe that you concluded on your own. This is why they sometimes won't outright make a rude statement, but they will make a disgruntled noise that leaves you questioning what you have just done and if it is still worthy of praise or validation. It sounds like a lot to take in, and it also seems very confusing—this is exactly right, and it is what your manipulator wants you to feel.

Standing firm in your actions will help you to avoid changing your opinions on yourself based on these negative speech patterns. If you know you did a good thing, you don't need validation from anyone to make it real—you can feel proud of yourself. The instant you realize that someone isn't happy for you or is trying to bring you down, this is a red flag that you must be aware of. No matter how long you have known this person and in what capacity, jealousy can fuel a lot of manipulative issues. Understand that your happiness does not depend on anyone else's reaction.

The easiest way to avoid tension during conversations like these is to relax your own facial expression and speak calmly at all times. Without breaking your stride, you will be able to say everything that you want to say without feeling forced to change your mind or your mood. If the other person is acting miserable or tense, this is not on you to fix. When you haven't done anything wrong, this becomes an attention-seeking behavior that they are using to try and lure you in. They want you to ask what is wrong so they can launch into their narrative.

Staying on topic when you are talking to a manipulator can be difficult because they are always trying to steer the conversation in a particular direction. When you are unwavering in your responses, this is going to frustrate them and thwart their plan. You might surprise them by acting in the exact opposite way that they are expecting, but this will keep you protected from their harmful energy. When you know that you do not have to put up with this, you will become more confident at maintaining your positive energy.

How to Handle Negative Body Language

1. **Seek Clarity**: Whenever you notice someone presenting you with negative body language, do not automatically assume that you have done something wrong—this is what they want you to think if they are manipulating you. Instead, seek a deeper reason for why this person might be acting this way. If you're going to address behavior without being confrontational, you can

say something like, "I'm sensing that you are uncomfortable." This statement is a prompt that gives the other person the change to explain how they feel. It is not your job to come up with this answer.

When you approach the situation this way, you are coming from a place of power. Instead of asking the person if they are mad at you or upset with you, it makes them think inwardly when you suggest that you are sensing that they are feeling discomfort. Pay close attention to the way they respond. They might come back with more defensiveness or maybe even a little bit of backlash. Remember to take their reaction with a grain of salt—their behavior will provide a tell-tale sign of what their intentions are and what they are thinking.

2. **Understand You Are Not a Mind Reader**: Accept that you are not always going to understand another person's body language. Since you cannot read minds, you might not have all of the information necessary to form a complete picture of what they mean. It is okay not to have all the answers. If you need more information from them, you need to ask them for it. When

you jump to conclusions or make assumptions, this puts you in a place where you might start to blame yourself for their negative body language—it is time to stop taking the blame for the things that are not your fault. You deserve to have clarity.

Try not to make everything about you. If you assume that someone is mad at you, consider that they might have been in a bad mood all day. Maybe they encountered an obstacle earlier that is still impacting them. Until you get a direct confirmation that someone is mad at you or upset with you, then you do not have to act like you have done anything wrong. The way that the other person thinks, regardless of if they are a manipulator or not, is not your decision to make. They are going to choose what they hold onto throughout the day, and this is going to impact their mood and communication style.

3. **Be Concise**: Regardless of how the other person is acting, you need to be clear about your intentions and how you express yourself. Speak clearly and honestly, only saying what you truly mean. You do not have to provide any additional explanations unless asked for themy.

This action will encourage you to stay true to your words. When it comes to your body language, keep it neutral if you do not know what to do. As mentioned, one of the best things you can do is to keep your arms relaxed and by your side with your body facing the person. Make eye contact, and keep your tone level. Your confidence is going to shine through when you do this.

You have complete control of the nonverbal communication you present to the other person, and the great thing is, you can adapt to a situation as it unfolds. If someone is incredibly rude to you, then you might not want to stand facing them or close to them. Use your best judgment and do what feels most natural. You do not have to keep up appearances just to make the other person feel a certain way. Your body language is a direct extension of the words you are saying. If someone tries to deconstruct your body language, do not let this catch you off guard. They might do this as an attempt to suggest they know exactly how you are feeling—only you know this, and you get to decide how much you want to share.

Chapter 4: Dark Neuro-Linguistic Programming

Neuro-linguistic programming, or NLP, refers to the idea of mind control. At first glance, this topic sounds very intimidating. The idea of somebody being able to influence your thoughts to the point where they can control you is scary and worrisome, but you will learn how to become aware of this practice and how to protect yourself from it. Richard Bandler and John Grinder invented the concept in the 1970s—it became popular during the 1980s through its occult standing. The topic was continually explored throughout the 1990s and early 2000s through advertisements, media, and politics.

Though the concept itself isn't new, it might feel new to you. How can you be sure that your mind isn't being controlled? The thing to remember is that NLP is not inherently bad. For example, companies use it in a lot of advertising that we see daily. Subliminal messages are scattered throughout commercials that encourage you to buy the product. You can refer to this simple strategy as NLP. What makes it dark is when someone tries to use this against you to take control of you for their gain. A manipulator loves to use this concept to their advantage because they are great at this style of communication. They will put an idea in your head that you will believe was your original thought.

As you become more aware of NLP, you will probably notice it more often. It is thought that NLP is a derivative of hypnotherapy in the way that it can put you into a sort of suggestive trance. Though you are not unconscious, your subconscious is still accessed in some way. We can define it as a technique where you layer subtle meaning on top of spoken or written language in an attempt to persuade someone to think a certain way. Without knowing that you are doing this, it seems like you could easily implant several suggestions into a person's mind by using this technique. Although most mainstream therapists reject the idea of NLP, it is something that others are very vocal about experiencing. No matter how you do it, the results are evident—when a person knows how to implement NLP correctly, they will be able to discover the following:

1. What side of a brain the person is using predominantly?
2. What sense is most prominent in their brain?
3. How does their brain use and store information?
4. Whether they are lying?

These are the positive uses of NLP. All of these factors are very helpful in trying to decode what someone might be trying to tell you. The dark element comes in when someone starts to use NLP on you to guide you in a direction that they want. This might be because it will negatively influence you, because it will positively influence them, or both. Either way, it becomes dark when the other individual's personal gain is at the top of the list of priorities.

Essentially, you can familiarize yourself with these techniques and use them to your advantage. At the very least, you are going to be able to protect yourself from dark NLP that manipulators try to use against you. It is great because you do not have to engage in a confrontation to stop dark NLP. Using very subtle techniques, you can be just as elusive as they are without them even realizing it. You no longer have to worry about people placing subliminal messages into your mind. From now on, only your real thoughts and feelings will be in your mind.

How to Protect Yourself

- **Become Aware of Mimicking**: If someone is mimicking you, take notice. Whether they are sitting in the same way as you or using the same words/speech patterns, this might be an indication that they are using dark NLP. Of course, mimicking happens naturally during communication for different reasons. There are ways to test them when you notice that they are copying you. Without making it very obvious that you are testing them, you can start by subtly moving your hands a certain way, maybe placing your fingers on top of your knuckles. See if they are doing the same thing as you, and see if they are watching your hands or your eyes.

Those who are deliberately mimicking you will make the same movement right away. You will notice their hands move almost instantly after you move yours. If this person is mimicking you naturally or out of habit without dark intentions, you might see them move their hands a little later in the conversation. In some ways, you have subconsciously impacted them, and they might move their hands based on the memory of you moving yours earlier.

At the very least, this becomes an interesting experiment that you can perform on just about everyone you communicate with. It becomes especially helpful if you feel that someone is trying to deceive you. Once you pick up on the fact that the person is doing this, it is almost comical when you catch them in the act. Do not call the individual out for what they are doing; it is better to keep this information to yourself for future use. You can simply observe them and then see if you feel that they are honest with you or if they have bad intentions.

- **Move Your Eyes a Lot**: This is something that can freak someone out who is trying to manipulate you by way of NLP. Since body language is frequently mimicked, moving your eyes in random or unpredictable patterns is an obvious indicator that the person is copying you. Slowly starting this technique off is the best way to go about it. If you begin by darting your eyes in all different directions, the individual might become confused or wary of your intentions. Maintain eye contact in the beginning, and then start to let your eyes wander.

Slowly looking in different directions will give you a chance to spot if the other person is doing the same thing. Look to the right, then left, and then right again.

This is a simple pattern that is not natural unless you are feeling worried or suspicious. It is definitely an eye contact pattern that you would not maintain in an average conversation. If the other person copies your pattern right away, you will be able to tell that they are intentionally copying you. With something this complex, a person who has good intentions is probably not going to mimic this behavior. They might end up asking you if you are okay instead.

- **Avoid Letting Them Touch You**: A casual touch during a conversation makes a conversation more intimate. Someone can touch you in a completely platonic way, but it is still possible that this can make you feel uncomfortable, especially if that person tries to use dark NLP against you. There is a theory that someone can "anchor" you by touching you. If you are in a state of distress or deep emotions, they might touch your shoulder to set up the anchor. Later on, they might touch you again in the same spot to trigger your mind and send you back into the same emotional state you were in before.

This is very similar to the story of Pavlov's dog. The

dog learned that he would get food each time he heard a bell ring—this is conditioning. In the same way that Pavlov trained his dog, a manipulator is just as easily able to condition you. This is the reason why keeping your distance during conversations will protect you from unwanted NLP. Without being close enough to touch you, the other person will never have the chance to anchor you. It ensures that you remain in full control of your emotions, and you never have to worry about if what you are feeling is natural or conditioned. This is an easy step to follow because touching of any kind needs to be consensual. If you are not comfortable with it, then you do not have to consent to it.

- **Be Aware of Vague Language**: When someone is speaking to you, take notice of how detailed they are with their speech. A significant technique of dark NLP is using vague language while speaking. This technique is thought to induce the other person into a hypnotic trance. If you have ever sat through a long, generalized lecture, then you know how easy it is to tune this kind of language out. Your mind ends up wandering, and maybe you even end up almost falling asleep. The same effect can happen when the person talking to you is being very vague. Though you aren't going to fall asleep in front of them, your brain mentally checks out.

Another thing that can happen when you hear very vague language is that you will become a lot less likely to disagree with anything. Because you can sense that the information is not very detailed, you are likely going to receive it more casually. Then, the other person can slip a subliminal message in there effortlessly and without you realizing it. You might mistakenly agree to something that you usually would not agree with because someone caught you off guard. It is a tactic used in dark NLP that tends to work very well because it gets our brains relaxed.

When the other person wants to take you out of the trance, all they have to do is start using precise language. It will perk you up and cause you to pay close attention. When they start describing things in great detail, your brain will re-engage. This forces you to pay attention on short notice, and it puts the other person in control of the conversation. Politicians will usually perform this technique when they give speeches.

- **Beware of Permissive Language**: You have probably been told at some point, "Feel free to relax." Make sure you watch closely for language that is permissive like this. While it can appear a kind gesture on the surface, there is a much deeper meaning to it when used by someone who is performing dark NLP on you. The best way to get people to do what you want is to give them "permission." Of course, you do not need anyone to tell you it is okay to relax. You will simply do so if you feel like relaxing. By telling you that you *can*, this implies that the other person has control over you. Without even thinking, you will respond positively to this prompt because it seems like the natural thing to do.

As you become more aware of these dark NLP tactics, make sure you are not blindly following the lead of someone else. If someone wanted to put you into a temporary trance to control your mind, all they would have to say is that you have permission to relax. Your brain hears those words, and you begin to let down your guard. You need to keep it up when you are talking to someone you do not trust, but do not let them know this. Someone who wants to control you will never deliberately say that they wish to place you in a trance, so there is no need to say that you are vigilant and resistant to their attempts. Keep this secret to yourself.

- **Take Note of Gibberish**: Have you ever been talking to someone, and they suddenly bring up a topic that you are entirely unaware of? Because you have no idea what they are talking about, this puts you into a position where you should just trust them because they seem to have more knowledge about the topic. Speaking gibberish is nothing more than a distraction that a manipulator wants you to fall for. There are several ways this can impact you. When you hear something you do not understand, you might feel inferior to the person you are talking to. Maybe you will experience confusion. No matter what, you are going to be distracted. This is the perfect opportunity for them to insert some subliminal messages because you are vulnerable.

Whenever this happens, you can combat it by simply asking them to elaborate. "Can you be more specific about that?" This question is an excellent way to counteract the gibberish because it is not an action that should result in conflict. By simply asking them to expand on their thoughts, you are calling them out for their gibberish. Manipulators are typically good at making up stories, so don't be surprised if they come back with something that almost seems to make sense. You are still going to be successful, however, because you did not fall for their trick. Your brain will still be very active and present in the foreground. Another thing to remember is that you are helping yourself out of any potential trance you might already be in. By forcing the person to use specific language, you will be transported back to reality.

- **Read Between the Lines**: When you are communicating with someone who might have bad intentions, you definitely need to read between the lines. This means that you must take everything into account, not only the words they are saying. You need to be aware of the context and body language. So much of what a manipulator says to you is layered with hidden messages or intentions. The sentences that are usually layered will come across as very obvious or straightforward. When you don't have a second thought about them, you are agreeable, which is exactly what the other person wants. It is another way to catch you off guard and to place thoughts into your head.

Someone might ask you something like, "Eating right, maintaining a diet, and sleeping with me are all very important, don't you agree?" If you were to glaze over this sentence and listen to it quickly, you would probably agree. The statement seems obvious, but the underlying message is deceiving. This is a way for the person to get to you unconsciously agree to certain things that you would normally not agree to. It is a dangerous tactic because it provides a false sense of consent. People who are very skilled with dark NLP are quick to come up with questions like these. Listen carefully when you are engaged in any conversation because you never know what you might be agreeing with. You are then going to be placed in a position where you must deny what you have already said, even if you didn't mean it at all.

- **Watch Your Attention**: This means that you need to be aware of how close you are paying attention. When you talk to someone who has malicious intentions of controlling you, they want you to take the most passive approach possible. The less you are paying attention, the more likely it will be that they can infiltrate your mind. You might zone out during conversations out of habit, but it is time to change this. When you pay close attention, you are protecting yourself.

Once you get the hang of paying attention, you can test the person to see what their true intentions are. Put on a front like you are not paying attention. You can do this by letting your eyes look down frequently or simply nodding slowly as the other person talks. Be very minimal with your responses. When they think they have you off guard, you can bounce back with a detailed answer that pertains to exactly what they are talking about—this will be sure to surprise them. An example might be if someone were talking about the best movies they have seen lately. You might nod along in agreement as they express how great this list of movies is. Once they think they have you zoned out, they might bring up a statement about how a certain film is superior because a man directed it. Thinking you are going to nod in agreement, you can retort with something witty that explains your stance on sexism in the movie industry. Their reaction should be priceless.

- **Stop Agreeing**: One of the easiest ways to protect yourself immediately is by refusing to agree with anything the other person is saying. You can do this in a way that does not come across as difficult or confrontational. The other person might be leading you into a conversation that forces you to give quick responses. These kinds of decisions come with the weight of a lot of pressure, even if they aren't significant ones. They might ask you to pick the best restaurant in town quickly, then later on, they will be able to complain about the food and the fact that you wanted to eat there.

When you find yourself in a situation that requires any kind of quick decision-making, you have every right to excuse yourself or to dismiss it. Be direct that you are not going to make the decision. That way, they won't have anything valid to blame on you. With a manipulator, they always want to have something they can negatively hold over you. If something bad happens based on a choice you make, this gives them a very easy transition into making you feel bad about yourself.

A good rule of thumb is to wait at least 24 hours before making any decision. This might seem like a long time, especially for something as simple as picking where to eat, but the thing is—this will require the other person to choose instead. If it is on a time crunch, they will become frustrated by your lack of participation and end up making a choice themselves. It is great because this is exactly what you want. It is their choice to make, so it becomes their responsibility.

- **Trust Your Intuition**: Your intuition guides you for a reason—always make sure you listen to it. If you've ever had a bad feeling about something, only to discover that it was true, this was your intuition warning you. When you feel that something isn't right or that someone is trying to take advantage of you, then you are probably right. These feelings do not arise out of thin air. Based on the energy that the person is providing, this is why you have come to this conclusion. There is nothing sudden about the assumption, even if it feels that way sometimes.

Most people who practice dark NLP are just going to seem "off." You might not even be able to accurately explain what is off about them or what they are doing wrong, but if you ever get that feeling, you should probably listen to it. You aren't necessarily in any kind of danger if you realize you are talking to a manipulator, but you need to be very careful about how much you give them. Do not allow them to take away any of your precious energy, and be sure to protect yourself by using the above techniques. You can only give them basic information that they will not be able to use against you. Do your best to avoid giving them any personal details or specific facts. They are going to sense your resistance to their dark NLP right away, but that doesn't mean they are going to give up. A manipulator enjoys a challenge, so you need to remain strong. Stand your ground, and always speak up if you notice that you are being forced into a situation you are not okay with.

Chapter 5: Brainwashing

You hear about it all the time. A person has been "brainwashed" to think a certain way. This type of mind control can cause people to do things that are out of character all the time and in significant ways. You might feel that you are immune to the act of being brainwashed because you are not weak, but even the strongest minds are still able to become brainwashed when they encounter the right manipulator. When you are brainwashed, you are essentially living a life that is not meant for you. It does not take into consideration your hopes, dreams, and desires. Instead, it is a path that has been chosen for you. Eventually, you will end up believing that this is the right option for you or that you came up with the idea yourself. It is a scary process that doesn't take long at all to infiltrate your brain.

There are several ways that you can become brainwashed. It is a pretty low likelihood that you will encounter a single person that has the ability to brainwash you completely, but there are definitely shady characters that will try. With a combination of political brainwashing and advertisement brainwashing, you will find yourself acting out in ways you never have before. One of the most interesting things is that you probably won't even realize you are doing it. When you are brainwashed, it is almost like you are being cut off from your subconscious. The only things you can think, say, or do are influenced by other people or events.

Brainwashing can occur for several months, even years. There are countless survivor's tales of people who have escaped from cults that they have spent almost their entire lives in because they thought it was what they were supposed to do. When someone else or something else has this much control over your brain, it is a scary thought. This is something that you need to avoid for your own safety and well-being. Having a solid support system is always going to help determine if you are acting out of character. If someone who knows you well expresses that you are different, it might be a good idea to explore what they are claiming.

Ask them to elaborate, and then evaluate yourself. Why are you acting this way? Have you ever acted this way before? If you haven't, what is causing you to do so now? Getting to the root of these situations by asking yourself questions is a great way to keep your brain active and involved. Understand that the people who care about you don't want to hurt or offend you. If they say that you are acting unlike yourself, they are coming from a place of concern. You should at least look into it by grounding yourself with those questions before you brush them off.

"You are the average of the five people you spend the most time with."
—Jim Rohn, American author, entrepreneur, and motivational speaker

When thinking about the above statement, would you say that this is true? Even if you are not exactly like a carbon copy of each of the five people you spend the most time with, it goes without argument that they influence your behaviors. You spend a lot of time with them because of what you have in common, so you are naturally like-minded. There might be stuff that you disagree on, but you will usually have a solid foundation with each of the five people you are around the most. Now, consider this—one of these five people are in a prime position to brainwash you.

The thought is not meant to make you paranoid or scare you, but it is a helpful way to view your reality. Think about how easy it would be to brainwash someone you already have a strong influence on. When your friend enjoys a certain restaurant, what do they do? They might tell you about it, aiming to convince you that it is a good restaurant. They might also take you to it, showing you just how good it is. Even if you do not care for the restaurant as much as they do, you will probably still agree to eat there occasionally because you know that they enjoy it so much. While this is a relatively benign example, the same exact method can convince you of other opinions.

There is usually an element of care involved—since you care about the other person's feelings or what they think, then you are probably going to come across as more agreeable than resistant. This is why manipulators are very quick to gain your trust. There is very little that someone can do to brainwash a complete stranger that they don't know anything about, but once they get to know you, they have some leverage to work with. Anyone who wants to brainwash you will try to learn as much about you as they can. They want to know exactly how your brain works, and they will be able to do this when you share your thoughts and opinions with them.

At any given point in time, you are agreeing with countless messages that are being fed to your brain. Some of this might be brainwashing on a level where the other person is well aware of what they are doing. By moving your thoughts back into your conscious brain, you will be able to avoid these tactics. Brainwashing is scary in its conceptual stage, but it is even more frightening when you do not know it is happening to you. As you navigate through life, you must know how to protect yourself from it on all scales. Do not put it past anyone that you know, especially those who are closest to you.

How to Avoid It

Now, you are going to learn how to avoid being brainwashed. These techniques also apply to situations that might be unfolding right now. It is not too late to regain control of your brain, and it is important that you have the desire to do so. You are a unique individual with valuable input and skills. You do not deserve to have anyone else deciding what you can and cannot do with your life. Through these methods, you will discover how to feel more grounded in your daily life. Without the influence of anyone or anything, you can rest easy knowing the decisions you are making are coming from your own desires.

Know Yourself

To know if someone is brainwashing you are or not, you must have a clear understanding of who you are as a person. This concept might seem funny or unnecessary to think about, but it is important. If you don't have a baseline to compare it to, then how will you ever know if someone else is controlling you? You need to have a solid grasp of what your core values are, the things that you truly believe in. These are the principles that you live your life by, and it is always a wise idea to revisit them from time to time. Understanding what is important to you will help you to become the best version of yourself.

Some examples of core values include the following:

- Loyalty
- Honesty
- Efficiency
- Reliability
- Commitment

These are traits that you might find desirable in another person, whether they are your partner or a platonic figure. You will also want to uphold them in your own life because you think they are so important. Having a strong set of core beliefs is a great thing, and knowing exactly what they are is important. If someone is making a statement that directly goes against one of your core beliefs, you will know when to speak up or what to do about it. You should never go along with something that forces you to feel like you are turning your back on your core beliefs—this is how brainwashing can begin.

To know yourself, you must also have an idea of what your basic likes and dislikes are. There might not be a real need to restate these messages, but for the sake of confirming that you are not being brainwashed, it is essential. Make a list of all the things you like. This list can include your favorite foods to eat and the activities that you like to participate in during your free time. Anything that you like can go on the list. Next, make a list of the things that you do not like. Next to each one, write down why you dislike it. This is a grounding moment for you because it confirms precisely what you do not like about each thing—it provides you with a sense of clarity.

Remember to go over what you are passionate about, as well. Your passions are the subjects you are willing to take action for. If you needed to take action, what is something that might make you react passionately? Your passions don't always have to be self-serving. Some people are naturally very caring, and they might enjoy doing nice things for other people. Humanitarian work is often a passion because it feels good to know you have made a difference in someone else's life. Try to focus on these things that matter most to you. Through this process of getting to know yourself again, you might realize you have changed—everyone does after some time. Change is not always a bad thing; it can signify growth. Nobody is going to be the same person they were 10 years ago. A lot can happen in that time. You might not even be the same person you were a few months ago. Our ever-evolving nature is why it is a good idea to revisit who you are and what you stand for frequently. It will keep you up to speed on your core values, current interests, and passions. By redefining who you are, you might even realize that you like yourself more than you used to in the past. You are a unique individual with many different skills and abilities—don't take this for granted.

Have a Vision for Your Life

When you have a clear vision of your purpose in life, this is a grounding experience. This likely means that you have goals that you are constantly working toward; you have a reason for doing what you do. It is hard to be swayed from a vision that means something to you. When you set goals for yourself and work hard to accomplish them, it is unlikely that you will simply walk away from this path that you are already on. While it is still possible, you are giving yourself a better chance of standing your ground by being mindful of your life goals.

If you haven't thought about what your goals are in a while, now is the perfect time to think about it again. As mentioned, a lot has probably changed since the last time you defined them. What are the things you want most in your life right now? What steps can you take to get there? These questions will guide you toward all of the right pathways that you can take. Having your goals in writing will make them even more powerful. When you can see a tangible list of goals that you are working toward, this will keep you motivated to accomplish them. It is easy to forget about your goals when you are only focusing on what is happening in the past or present—you need to have some plans for your future, too. Knowing what you want to do with your life can be difficult, no matter how old you are or what stage you are in life. This is why having both short-term and long-term goals will help you. Short-term goals are the ones you can see yourself accomplishing in under three months. They are going to happen fairly soon, and they are probably relatively high on your list of priorities. You can take daily action to make these goals happen. Long-term goals probably have a deadline that is further away. These goals can take longer to accomplish because they are more demanding or because time must permit. No matter the reason, it is good to have a mix of both on your list.

Keep yourself engaged by staying motivated. If you always have a goal to work on, then you are going to be able to stay focused. Make sure you break each goal down into manageable steps. If you set yourself up for failure, this will only discourage you and make you feel like there is no purpose in your life. This is a prime opportunity for someone else to come in and influence your behaviors. Have faith in yourself and in your ability to reach your goals, no matter what they are. When you feel like giving up, find a smaller milestone that you can reach, and then reward yourself. You deserve to be acknowledged when you do a great job, and you do not have to wait for anyone else to validate you.

Be Curious

Most of the time, it is easy to move about your life without thinking twice about it. You form routines to help you complete tasks in an efficient manner. Through these routines, you feel stable and secure. While they can offer you a lot when it comes to organization and productivity, they also keep you within certain constructs. It is only when something outside of your routine happens, usually bad, that you think about changing up your routine. Instead of waiting until an event happens to change your routine, you can do something about this sooner—commit to making small changes daily. Even if this simply involves eating your breakfast in a different room, you are still making a change. When you begin to think outside of the box, you will approach deeper topics, like your life path and career options. A lot of people can become brainwashed into thinking that what their life currently entails is all that they deserve. Some people believe they have reached a final stage of sorts—this isn't true because there is always more to be done if you want a change in your life. You can completely transform the way you think and behave to reinvent your lifestyle entirely.

Exercising your curiosity helps with breaking the constructs of your routines. Have you ever wondered how your loved ones live their lives? You can see it happening in front of you, but have you ever thought about the tasks they perform on a daily basis? Feeling this type of curiosity will get you thinking about possibly trying some of these new methods. Because they can be a lot different than what you are used to, you might discover some interesting ways to achieve the same results more efficiently.

Being curious also puts you at a lower risk of being brainwashed. If you are constantly changing what you are doing, there is little room left for any manipulation to try to convince you that you do not have options. Through the small changes you make regularly, you will have first-hand experience of all the options that are available to you. The great part about life is that you are not the only factor in it. Other people, places, and situations surround you. All of these components come together to form your reality. If even the slightest change is made by anyone or anything, a new array of possibilities becomes available.

Think about all of the problems you are currently facing. Consider how long you have been stuck on them and why. With a little curiosity, you will be able to form a new path to follow. The situations that once hindered you and limited you will no longer stand in your way. You will see that you can also avoid toxic people if need be—a notable skill to have when trying to avoid being brainwashed. The time to start these changes is right now. The longer you wait, the more you are delaying your potential for progress.

Remain Open But Grounded

When you have an open mind, this means you have the ability to be humble—you understand that there is always more to learn. This quality is excellent to have because you are aware that you do not know everything. If someone presents you with new information, you do not have to take it in as factual information automatically. Be open-minded to the fact that it might be, but also remain aware that it might not. This is a great way to explore your life.

Seek out new information whenever you can. This does not mean you have to teach yourself new languages or skills to enhance your abilities. You can simply watch new movies, read different books, and try unfamiliar foods. All of these actions are going to broaden your life experiences in unique ways. If someone provides you with a suggestion, you do not always have to take it. The choice is yours, and this is how you will remind yourself that you can be both open and grounded.

Focus on what is truly interesting to you. Part of knowing exactly who you are comes from discovering what you enjoy doing and what you like. If you are interested in a particular hobby, see what you can do to take it to the next level. Learn about its history or teach yourself a new technique. There are many ways to spruce up old concepts without having to relearn anything completely. This measure will help you when it comes to brainwashing because you will become quick-thinking. Having the ability to consider many possibilities while continuing to stay firm within your beliefs is a great quality to have.

It's easy to stray from who you truly are and what you believe in because of others' influence, but you can work on regaining that strength. When you have a solid foundation of who you are as a person, this allows you to stay true to who you are. It is human nature to want to be included, which is why it is so tempting to jump on all of the bandwagons and to follow the latest trends. Sometimes, these are not the behaviors that truly align with who you are. Even if you have different interests, you can still find others who you share commonalities with.

The key to avoid being brainwashed by the masses is to be aware of it before it happens to you. When you notice that something is rising in popularity, consider why this is happening. See if you can identify with the trend and if you want to participate for a genuine reason. If you do not, this does not mean you must alienate yourself from any group or society. Your unique qualities will shine through, and you will attract like-minded people into your life by being genuine.

Chapter 6: Mind Control

Mind control is an aspect of manipulation that is similar to brainwashing. The main difference is that the individual might only want to control your mind at the moment. Maybe they want to get you to do something that will benefit them temporarily because they are opportunistic individuals. Since there is not much time to take over a person's mind when you are engaged in a simple conversation, there are some very detailed techniques that a manipulator will use to attempt to gain control of your mind. As you explore these techniques, you will also learn how to combat each of them. The stronger your mind is, the better you will be at warding off the people trying to harm you.

Compensating for Lack of Physical Prowess

Someone might try to control your mind because you secretly intimate them. Because they do not appear physically threatening, a manipulator will be quick to move forward with mind control by seeing how much they can change your thoughts. The mind control gives them the same type of satisfaction they would receive if they were physically controlling you. Because the latter is a lot more obvious, the idea of controlling your mind is also a lot more appealing.

You will find that manipulators are very discreet about this. They might remark at how strong or tough you are, building you up based on your physical characteristics. Even a simple comment about you being tall can be enough to let you think that they respect you because you have more physical prowess than they do—this is exactly what they want you to think. Instead of backing down, which is what you will think they are doing, they make you more vulnerable by making you comfortable.

When you believe that someone sees powerful traits in you, then you are going to be less likely to assume that they have bad intentions. Surely because they appear to respect you, they won't deceive you, right? Always make sure that you remind yourself anyone can fool you at any time. It is hard to keep track of everyone's true intentions, especially when they have mastered the art of mind control.

What You Can Do: Remain firm in your core beliefs. Even if you believe that the individual respects you and what you stand for, always remind yourself of what you hold dear to your heart. By staying true to who you are, this gives you little reason to change your opinions on a whim. Remind yourself that the person trying to control your mind is very insecure.

Using Hand Placement as a Decoy

Have you ever noticed that people normally place their fingers on their heads when thinking very hard? In moments of concentration, you have probably done the same thing. This is a subconscious mind control technique that is often used by manipulators. When they want you to rethink something, they might place their fingers on their head to coax you into doing the same. With the help of muscle memory, your brain will be receiving a message that it needs to think harder.

It is an interesting technique because it is so subtle. You surely would not notice it if you were not looking for it in the first place. As you become better at reading body language, you will become more aware of moments when the person you are talking to is merely using a decoy movement as an attempt to control you. Do your best to break the mirroring effect that typically happens during a conversation. Keep your arms in a neutral position by your side.

Manipulators get nervous. In fact, they probably get very nervous and will do the best they can to hide this from you. As soon as you notice their fingers move up to their head, imagine that they are nervous that they won't be able to pull off this attempt at mind control. Pride yourself in your ability to pick up on it before it affects you—this will keep you strong.

What You Can Do: In an attempt to break their cycle, you can make a comment that indirectly refers to them concentrating. Something like, "Oh, is that what you were thinking?" is a way to make manipulators second-guess their abilities. If you let them know from the start that you are not automatically going to agree with what they are saying, this will be your way of standing your ground.

Convincing You of Psychic Powers

The person who is manipulating you is not any more powerful than you—repeat this to yourself often. Even though many mind controllers are portrayed as psychic beings, this is not the case for most. A successful manipulator is usually just very good at picking up on your body language and context. There is nothing psychic about it, though it can definitely feel that way at times.

Being misinformed that someone is psychic and can read your mind at any time is intimidating. These are your private thoughts, and you do not want anyone intruding upon them. The good news is that you never have to let this happen. You are still in control of your inner thoughts, and what you share with the world is always going to be your decision. Anyone who tries to force you or to coax you into sharing something you do not want to does not have your best interest at heart. The mention of psychic abilities might come up as a joke. For example, the manipulator will joke around with you while mentioning that you don't need to say much because they already know what you are thinking. You can laugh this off, but you can also remain firm in your belief that this isn't true. With the way you portray yourself, you can get them to think anything you want.

What You Can Do: Always be aware of your intention during every conversation. If you are presenting yourself in a certain way, the manipulative person is going to pick up on it. Try your hardest to practice standing neutrally and speaking neutrally. When you can master this concept, it will be a lot harder for them to read you.

Surrounding You with Other Manipulative People

This is an especially dangerous mind control technique because it closely ties in with the idea behind brainwashing. The more people that you believe are on the same page about something will make you want to agree with them, too. If a manipulator can find other people who want to manipulate a vulnerable person, you might become an easy target for a bad situation. They will gang up on you in a way that is subtle yet effective. You do not have to put up with this. Knowing who you are as a person will protect you in many ways.

There will be times when a manipulator will only "scout" for like-minded individuals that believe in the point they are making. Unknowingly, they might recruit innocent bystanders to further lead you into thinking that you must agree with them. The people that also fall victim to these traps might be people you love and respect. This is why it might be tempting to give in and to just "go with the flow." It is exactly what the manipulator wants you to think. They want others to know that it is easier to go with a mass opinion rather than forming their own.

What You Can Do: Speak up when you disagree with something. This is difficult because you do not want to cause conflict or controversy, but it becomes necessary to protect yourself. A disagreement does not always have to turn into an argument. If you approach the situation maturely, you can simply speak your mind to get your point across without requiring validation. You can provide this for yourself. Remind yourself that it is not their opinions that matter most. Your view of yourself dictates your self-esteem.

Believing it Won't Happen to You

Because a mind controller works hard to use other people, you might assume that they would rather do this to strangers or bystanders. One of the most challenging realities to face is that these individuals are more likely to attempt the act of mind control on a loved one. This happens because the task seems a lot easier—they already know you well. Instead of having to figure out the things that get under your skin, they have an idea of what to say and how to persuade you. Realizing this can be very hurtful, especially when you have a lot of trust invested in the person.

"I would *never* do anything to hurt you," is a promise that is often broken by a manipulator. With mind control, they are directly going against that promise, even if it doesn't feel hurtful at the moment. When someone does not respect you for who you are, they will do anything to change you. Suggesting you should get something else to eat or that you should shop elsewhere for clothing are two simple examples of how manipulators can use their conviction to change you. You might not believe that these little changes mean much, but when you add them up, they can completely transform who you are as a person. It is not a great feeling to realize that you no longer recognize who you are. As upsetting as it is, you have to work on rebuilding yourself and getting back to your roots. It is normal to feel betrayed because this is what the manipulator has done to you—betrayed your trust.

What You Can Do: Never let your naive thinking get in the way of your rational thinking. You are not immune to the mind control that goes on around you. Your strength does not necessarily protect you from the intentions of all manipulators. By keeping yourself humble, you will always be on alert for the red flags presented by those who wish to change your mind.

The Blank Stares of Intimidation

Making a statement to someone and receiving a blank stare in return is intimidating for many reasons. One of the most prominent is that you do not know what they are thinking. It scares you because you might not know what to say or do next. A manipulator will use this technique to control your mind after you have said something vulnerable or profound. This will make you second-guess if what you said was "wrong" or incorrect somehow. You will end up prioritizing their feelings over your own.

They might follow this instance up with a statement that seems wise or all-knowing. When you combine the two actions, you are sure to believe that they can read your mind or that they know something you don't know. Both possibilities are unsettling in their own ways. When you feel a negative emotion, understand that this is what your manipulator wants you to feel. They want to catch you off-guard and make you question everything that you have confirmed in your reality. By slowly breaking you down and staring at you blankly, you will get the idea that you came to this conclusion independently. It becomes maddening when you do not realize what is happening to you.

What You Can Do: Always remind yourself that your feelings are valid. Even if you cannot explain them right away, you are feeling them for a reason. Explore these reasons with yourself, and truly get in touch with your emotions. Having a lot of emotional maturity is a great way to protect yourself from mind control. A manipulator is not going to be able to access your deepest thoughts unless you want them to. Keep them to yourself until you know you are talking to somebody trustworthy.

Off-Putting Energy Won't Always Equate to Mind Control

When you encounter someone that you define as "creepy," you are going to feel biased against them. If you were given a chance to choose between spending your time with a loved one and spending your time with a creepy person, the choice seems obvious. The scary part is that it is not only those who exude bizarre energy who want to control your mind. Some people are naturally going to rub you the wrong way, but they won't always have malicious intent behind their bizarre behavior.

You must learn the difference between your energy preferences and the intentions of others. While the two might end up overlapping at some point, you cannot automatically assume that someone is going to behave a certain way because of their resting energy. This is where spotting a mind controller becomes difficult. It takes a combination of common sense and energetic sense to weed out the people in your life who you no longer feel comfortable being around.

To distance yourself from somebody in your life does not require an excuse or a detailed explanation. If you find that a person is trying to control your mind, you do not owe them any favors, as they were just betraying you. Putting distance between this energy and your own will help to kickstart the healing process.

What You Can Do: Stay far away from those you do not get along with. You can be civil with almost anyone, but this does not mean you have to form any type of friendship or even acquaintanceship. The thing about any relationship is that it does not need to be defined by a label or by a level—it can simply just *be*. If you are not comfortable with a person's energy and cannot avoid them, try to balance it out by exuding more of your positive energy.

Lowering Your Heightened Awareness

When a manipulator realizes that you are onto them, they won't always stop with their attempts at mind control. It might motivate them to work even harder and smarter. Never let anyone bring you down from your sense of awareness. It is a big red flag to reach a point of enlightenment, only to be convinced by someone else that it is not important or it does not matter. Those who care about you are always going to support what you care about. When someone tries to convince you otherwise, they probably have ill intentions in mind.

You should feel proud of your awareness because it is not easy to maintain. Once you figure out what it takes to recognize all of the signs and signals of mind control, the next step is to make sure you don't forget how. A master manipulator is great at changing your mind, even when it comes to lessons you think you have already learned. As a rule of thumb, there is never anything wrong with giving yourself some reminders. Cycle through the reasons why being aware is better than being led blindly astray.

Mind control is a lot easier to perform when the mind is already slightly weakened. This is what a manipulator aims to do when they lower your sense of awareness. They want you to act like a sheep, only following their instructions and relying on their guidance unknowingly. If you ever need to check up on the strength of your mind, think about your morals. These are the principles you live your life by. If someone were to violate one of them, visualize what you would say and do.

What You Can Do: Boost yourself up in private. If you can uplift yourself without the help of anyone else, you have reached a great point of awareness. You will realize that your happiness should not revolve around anyone but yourself. Continue to support this theory by always doing your best to validate yourself. You can do this by celebrating your successes and realizing that you have a lot of fantastic qualities.

Mind Control Isn't an End-All

If you do end up being controlled by another person, even if it continues for years, you can still break free from the cycle. It is a guarantee that you have been persuaded by someone else on multiple occasions throughout your life. You cannot be hard on yourself or believe in the idea that you will never be able to think for yourself again. The mind is flexible and durable. You are not the same person you were a year ago—consider all that has changed.

Because your mind is always evolving, so are your thoughts. What you believe in one moment can easily be changed in the next. The manipulator wants you to think that you have no escape once they have already controlled you, but you are much stronger than they give you credit for. Your mind can evolve, and you can learn how to harness all of the above techniques to protect yourself from any future potential of mind control.

What You Can Do: Forgive yourself. The most important part of moving on is forgiveness, and you need to include yourself in this process. If you realize that someone in your life has been controlling your mind, this is an upsetting discovery. You cannot blame yourself and your actions. Instead of thinking about what you could have done, focus on the present. What will you do if you are in the same situation again? This is how you can take what has happened to you and turn it into a valuable life lesson.

Chapter 7: Toxic/Harmful Relationships

Any relationship can be toxic if it hurts you. When a person knowingly makes decisions that upset you or make you feel uncomfortable, this is incredibly harmful to your well-being. On both a physical and emotional level, you by the toxic relationships you encounter impact you severely. Not only will they leave you with a lot of pain to heal from, but they will also skew your perspective on what is healthy and what is unhealthy. It can be complicated to figure out who is treating you right and who is taking advantage of you, especially after reading about all of the ways that a person can deceive you. This chapter is meant to provide you with some clarity. You will be able to evaluate all of the relationships in your life, platonic and otherwise, to ensure that others treat you the way you deserve.

The following traits can define a toxic relationship:

- It always feels bad, even if you are not fighting with the person.
- You are continually bracing yourself for an outburst.
- You avoid expressing your true feelings.

- They do not put any effort into the relationship.
- All of the loving energy comes from you.
- You feel like you cannot say "no" to them.
- They keep track of how many times you are wrong.
- When you are in a challenging situation, you find yourself lacking their support.
- They have passive-aggressive tendencies.
- There are moments of physical or verbal abuse.

To further explore the health of the relationships you keep, it is a good idea to take a closer look at each of these traits. If you can relate to any of them, even just one, this might indicate that your relationships need some reworking. Consider that you can save some of them, but if a person is truly just using you and manipulating you, there will be little hope unless they come to this conclusion on their own. No matter how much you wish you could change or help a manipulator, that responsibility is not on you. They need to feel responsible for their actions.

You Cannot Shake a Bad Feeling

Whenever you spend time with someone in your life, you are left with a feeling. This is a lasting impression of that person's energy. If you constantly feel like there is something bad looming, you likely feel like you cannot escape the bad energy. For some reason, this person is causing you to feel bad or uncomfortable. It is important to recognize these signs because you need to get to the root of them to solve the problem. Once you figure out precisely what they are doing that you do not like, you will be able to go over all of your options.

At times, the reasons will be obvious—this person might put you down by belittling you. Name-calling is another trait that can appear in an abusive relationship. Even if profanity is not used, when someone calls you a name that makes you feel weak or ashamed, this is unhealthy. If you can clearly see a pattern of disrespectful behavior, you need to use this as your motivation to break free from the situation. Leaving isn't easy, especially when feelings are involved, but it is for your safety and benefit. It is okay to put yourself first.

A toxic person will always try to make themselves the center of attention. If they feel upset or unhappy, they will let you know all of the things you did to contribute to their feelings. However, when you feel the same way, they won't be willing to listen to a word of what you have to say. Understand that their feelings are not any more valid than your own—you are worthy of being acknowledged and valued by everyone you allow into your life.

The Outbursts Are Frequent

If you feel like the person can snap at any given moment and it will all be your fault, this is unhealthy. You might get upset, but you can successfully rationalize what is causing your problem and how to go about fixing it. A toxic person isn't going to do this kind of emotional digging. Their first response will be finding someone else to place the blame on. If you are a person who is close to them, this makes you a huge target.

You deserve to live your life without living in fear over how someone else might react to what you do. This is that feeling of constantly walking on eggshells because you never know what willplease them and what will set them off. The thing about toxic people is that they tend to be unpredictable—even when you think you have them all figured out, they will have an outburst that will be sure to confuse you even further.

Instead of scrambling around trying to figure out ways to make them happy, you need to learn how to let go of the idea that you are responsible for their happiness. The only happiness you are responsible for is your own—seek it and live a life that serves you well. If they complain about it or have an outburst, remind yourself that you are not at fault. It might take time to learn how to let go of this fear because outbursts are scary. You never know what might set off a toxic person or how badly they will react. Naturally, this can lead you to develop many fears surrounding expressing yourself and staying true to who you are.

Your Feelings Come Last

If you are in a toxic relationship, you are likely conditioned into thinking that your feelings are less than the other person's. With this being said, they will continuously react how they want to react and expect you to accept them fully. If you ever have a bad day or want to complain, they will make you feel bad about this self-expression. When you put these two factors together, you are probably going to turn inward when it comes to saying what you are truly thinking and feeling what you are truly feeling.

They want you to feel wrong about how you feel so they can manipulate you into believing that they matter more. This is not a way that you should accept to be treated, no matter who this person is to you. Most of the time, toxic relationships are romantic, but this is not an exclusive trait. You can have a toxic relationship with a family member, your best friend, a coworker, or your boss. Because toxicity is a learned behavior, virtually anyone in your life can become a toxic person.

No matter the situation you are in, you deserve to be heard. When you express your feelings, you do not need to feel irrelevant or less than. If anyone is trying to convince you of this, it is probably stemming from their deep-rooted insecurities. Since they need extra help convincing themselves that they matter, they will try to bring others down. Even if they claim they love you and care about you, these actions will say otherwise.

It can sometimes feel easier just to keep your mouth shut instead of speaking up about your feelings when others treat you this way. Even though it is tiring and discouraging, you need to continue to express yourself. Remind yourself that you are still valid, even without their approval. When they can convince you that you are not worthy, it will become tough for you to break free from their toxicity because it will become your new version of normal.

Their Effort is Nowhere to Be Found

To put effort into a relationship is not always going to be a grand gesture. The person does not need to declare their love for you in an impressive way or buy you gifts to show you that they value your friendship, but there needs to be some effort present. If you are left wanting more from the relationship, then your needs are not being met. There is a way that you can put this person to the test. Figure out if they are simply unaware that they are not meeting your needs or if they do not care. Speak up about the fact that your needs aren't being met, and explain what you desire. Anyone who truly cares about you will want to fix the problem. A manipulator will likely get defensive or angry with you.

You do not need to put up with any minimal effort relationships, especially when you always give other people your all. The easiest way to remove yourself from them is to stop giving. When you do not offer them anything to take, this is going to send a message that you are onto the fact that they are using you. It might be difficult to change your behavior because you are so used to giving, but you have to understand that you are eventually going to run out of anything to give away. Pretty soon, you will become a shell of the person you once were.

To protect yourself from this kind of toxicity, you need to fully acknowledge when someone is not putting in as much effort as you are. Whether you are romantically involved or otherwise, effort is essential. No single person should be holding up the entire relationship on their own because this is incredibly tiring and unfair.

You Keep the Love Alive

Being a naturally kind person is a beautiful thing, but you might ignore some key signs of a toxic relationship when you are used to giving all of the love. If you care for someone, you will want to help them at any chance you get. This will include dropping your own needs in favor of what the other person needs. It is not necessarily a sign that the person is toxic, but you need to compare what you do for them with what they do for you. Do not count the times when they *say* they would do anything for you because actions speak a lot louder than words. See if you can pinpoint the last time that they did anything for you out of the kindness of their own heart and not because you asked.

Even if they are closely following your requests and attempting to meet your desires, a relationship needs to have mutually beneficial qualities. When you tell them exactly what to do and how to do it, you are still putting all of the efforts into the relationship. It is okay to help people out when they do not know what you need, but you should not have to constantly guide them in the right direction. If they truly care about you, they will be willing to explore how to figure it out—this is what makes a great relationship dynamic.

Though you can keep the love alive on your own, this does not mean you have to. Only give your love to those who are deserving of it. The great part is, you get to decide who these people are. By hand-selecting those who you are closest to and who you trust, you will be able to tighten your inner social circle. Try to fairly judge whether or not each person in your life you care for also cares for you in the same way.

Saying "No" Feels Taboo

It can be challenging to say no to anyone you care about, but it becomes a problem when that person makes it feel like you do not have a choice. You are always within your right when you say no. It doesn't matter what is happening or what the context is—if you want to say no, this is a sign that you are no longer comfortable with what is happening. It doesn't matter if you originally agreed to the situation. Once you get into it and you realize you are no longer okay with it, then you can still say no. This same concept applies if you are free to do someone a favor but you do not want to—just say no. The concept of saying no is a lot easier than the action itself. You are fearful of the judgment or backlash you will receive, and this is understandable. What happens when you say no is you get to take back some of your power. Just because you have the time, energy, or concentration to do something for someone does not mean you *have* to do it. You will learn how to value yourself, not wishing to push yourself to the point of burnout. Even if the other person reacts unfavorably, you didn't owe them anything to begin with.

In a close relationship situation, the person might try to use your status to guilt-trip you. Because you are their romantic partner or sibling or best friend, they feel that you should want to perform these requests. Do not let this deter you. If they care about you so much, then they should understand when you are uncomfortable or when you no longer have anything left to give. You should never give all that you have because this leaves you with nothing left for yourself.

They Are Always Keeping Score

Nobody is perfect—repeat that statement. If you feel that this individual is constantly reminding you of when you are wrong and of times in the past when you have been wrong, this is a problem. You should never feel that you are being put on the spot, let alone being judged in this way by a person who is supposed to have compassion for you. The reasoning behind why they keep score is a lot deeper than you think. They don't only want to make you aware of their imperfections; they want to use these moments to their advantage when you are wrong again.

Have you ever been in an argument with someone who tries to bring up mistakes you have made in the past that do not relate to the current conversation? This is what a manipulator will try to do when they have you in a toxic relationship. Anything that you have ever gone gets put up on the chopping block, and you are lucky if you can get a word in edgewise. They will try to make you feel so bad that you simply give in to whatever they are telling you—this destroys your self-esteem over time.

Countering their toxicity by bringing up past woes that they have made isn't the answer either. By doing this, you are only stooping down to their level. To truly rise above their criticism, you must have confidence in yourself and in who you are as a person. If you know that you are a good person who learns from every mistake you make, you will also know that the opinions of others are irrelevant to this factor. Nobody should be able to make you feel like you are lesser than.

When You Are Going Through Something, They Are Nowhere to be Found

Life is hard, and this is an understatement. You consistently try to be there for those you care about, offering your support in any way you can deliver it. When you care about someone deeply, you are going to be especially helpful to them as you will offer them both physical and emotional support that will aim to alleviate their pain. This is a trait that most good people have, and it shows a lot of compassion and nurturing. What happens when you are in a tough spot? If you notice that you do not get any support from this particular individual, this is definitely a sign of toxicity. The unequal level of care is going to sting a lot when you realize that they aren't there for you in the same way you are for them. It might make you feel upset or angry because of all the time you had invested in them when they were feeling down, and it should. You deserve to be treated with mutual love and support from those you consider closest to you. Not being able to rely on your partner, or anyone else very close to you, during a hard time is toxic. It becomes harmful because you feel that you need to deal with these issues and burdens on your own. You might end up feeling completely overwhelmed, and you might also realize that the other person does not want to hear about your struggles. This experience can lead you to suppress your thoughts and emotions, which is unhealthy. It is merely a different way for you to hold onto them without addressing them.

By Default, They Are Passive-Aggressive

The ability to be passive-aggressive is one that many toxic individuals share. They can make you feel like you have done something wrong without coming right out and saying it directly. This type of manipulation works well because it plays off your weaknesses. If they know that you are impacted by animals that do not have to eat, they might rattle off a quick statement like, "It's a shame that you didn't stop to feed that dog…Now he is probably going to feel hungry tonight." This is only one example of how manipulators might work in their passive-aggressive tendencies.

They will use this trait in arguments almost every time. It forms a distraction that they can rely on instead of taking accountability for their issues. They might "casually" bring up some faults that you have but then make you feel like they are okay with them. This is damaging for many reasons, and you end up feeling like you are the only one in the wrong. You might also end up feeling like you have to change who you are because you are not good enough for them. When, in reality, it is them that needs to change.

You cannot change a manipulator, and you should not try. They are going to do anything they can to get what they want, and if being passive-aggressive is what they choose, you need to learn how to look out for the signs so you can become more aware of it. Any time you feel that the conversation has suddenly flipped to make you feel bad about yourself, this is likely a moment when they are being passive-aggressive toward you. If you know you have done nothing wrong, then you know that there is little truth behind what they are saying and what they are attempting to get you to feel.

Abuse is Always Uncalled For

If someone is abusing you, you do not need to justify why or how it happens. Abuse is always something that you should not put up with, whether it is in the physical or the verbal form. When someone is abusing you, this puts you in a dangerous situation that might be difficult for you to escape from. By having so much control over you, the manipulator is able to get into your mind by hurting you and putting you down. You might feel that this is exactly what you deserve, even if it is far from the truth.

Abuse is very serious, and it should always be treated that way. Even if you feel that others have it worse than you, this does not negate the fact that you do not deserve to be treated this way. Reach out to someone you can trust when it is safe to do so. By telling at least one person about the abuse occurring, you have a chance of being able to form a plan that will allow you to safely remove yourself from the situation.

If you confront an abuser, their tendencies might end up flaring up—this puts you in a lot more danger. You need to be strategic when you form your plan. Make sure you have a safe place to go if you decide you need to physically leave. Your abuser might follow you or come to your new dwelling to continue the abuse. If necessary, you need to make sure that you are ready to call the police once you get yourself safely distanced from this person. Getting help is very scary, not only because someone is abusing you, but because you do care a lot for this person. It isn't wrong to feel this way, as they presented themselves as someone you could trust.

Chapter 8: The Three Personalities

You have learned a lot about dark psychology and manipulation techniques. There are so many ways that another person might try to use you or control you, but you are becoming familiarized with their methods to prevent this from happening. It is crucial to recognize that someone's personality type is important because this can distract from the bigger picture of what is happening. There are three main personality types that abusers and manipulators typically identify with. By spotting the people who function this way, you might be able to avoid their dark psychology techniques before you even formally introduce yourself.

As you "get to know" each personality, see if you can identify anyone in your life currently who fits these descriptions. It will prove to be an insightful evaluation, as most people know at least one of the three at any given moment. In an effort to further protect yourself, you will be able to identify and learn how to deal with each of the personality types described below.Empowering yourself with this information will allow you to feel safer and protected when you are opening up to those around you.

The personality types to identify are narcissists,

Machiavellians, and psychopaths—known as the dark triad in psychological terms. Each one has its own unique properties, but they share many commonalities. Because they are closely linked, knowing which type you are dealing with is super important. Fully understanding if you are interacting with someone who is a part of the dark triad will allow you to figure out what you need to do next. Without panicking or fumbling, you will be able to navigate your way with each one successfully.

Narcissist

The main characteristics:

- Domination
- Expressionism
- Exploitation
- Superiority
- Entitlement

This type of personality is very dynamic, and surprisingly, many people find themselves drawn to narcissists. They are able to convince you that they are trustworthy, so you will feel comfortable opening up to them. By the time you realize that they do not have your best intentions in mind, it might be too late to break free from their tactics.

A narcissist might appear as a very confident individual. For this reason, you are probably going to be intimidated by them right away. They always seem to know what they are doing and how to do it, but this is only a mask they are wearing to hide their deep-rooted insecurity. No matter what the situation is, a narcissist will attempt to reach a point of personal gain. They do not care if they have to put others down in the process, even their loved ones.

When a narcissist describes themself, they will likely have a lot of good things to say. They might even exaggerate their talents and skills in an effort to impress those around them further. To a narcissist, they truly believe they are the best and are worthy of endlesspraise—this attention is what fuels them in life. They like to be acknowledged and recognized for their greatness, even when it makes others feel bad about themselves and when it is not entirely true.

Narcissists do not like relationships or connections that are not beneficial right away. They do not want to spend a lot of time getting to know you and learning your interests. Instead, they will learn just enough to get close to you so they can use you. Narcissists are all about quick returns and instant gratification—they do not have the patience to take things slow with you. This is one reason why many people find themselves in romantic relationships with narcissists. In the beginning, it might seem like they have a lot of passion for you because they want to move quickly. What this ends up doing is making you open up to them faster. This result is exactly what they want because they are using you for attention or personal gain.

A narcissist is likely to be a cheater because this is one example of a situation that will present them with instant gratification. Rather than working toward the long-term relationship they are already in for the hope of a happy future, they will act on their impulses and make choices that allow them to experience the most benefits. You cannot trust a narcissist, no matter how much they make it seem like they are charismatic and trustworthy—this is exactly what they want you to think.

How to Deal with One

It is important never to push a narcissist. Pushing isn't going to change them, nor will it help your dynamic. While it seems counterproductive to accept a narcissist, this is one of the best things you can do. When you accept them, this gives them a reason to believe that you have already fallen for their trap. The great thing is, you can still be aware of their narcissistic personality without allowing them to control you.

If you simply let them think that you are okay with who they are, you will become less of a target on their radar. Any resistance from you will likely be met with backlash from them.

While this doesn't seem like the best approach, it is definitely one that works and keeps you more protected than if you were to open yourself up to a narcissist. You can still set firm boundaries when you take this stance by saying no to them and fighting for what you believe in. If they are trying to make you do something that you are not okay with, they cannot control you—the power is yours to walk away or to decline the suggestion. Once you experience how great it feels to take back this power, you will no longer be afraid of saying no to a narcissist.

To make the task easier, you should always expect the worst. If you push a narcissist, they will most definitely push back. The thing about this is that you can soften the blow by predicting that this will happen. If you are not 100% agreeable, they might lash out at you. As long as you are not in physical or emotional danger, you can simply accept this and move forward. They want you to react or become debilitated, but you do not have to give them the satisfaction. Remember that you are a great person, even despite any insults or backlash that comes your way. They might try to bring you down, but if you can remember the truth, you will be just fine. Find support from the people who truly care about you, and get all of your feelings out about the issue when you are no longer in the presence of the narcissist. Opening up to them will not fix any of the problems they have. Narcissism can turn into a severe illness that requires professional help to get through.

If you feel that you are in a safe position to do so, you can tell them directly that their behavior is damaging or harmful and why. Keep in mind that this is probably going to result in an outburst, but even the most straightforward message might strike a chord within that inspires change. As long as you are not holding onto hope that they will change, it can be very empowering to speak up and describe precisely why their behavior is not okay. This puts you in a more powerful position, and the individual will realize that they cannot easily control you any longer.

Machiavellian

The main characteristics:
- Self-interest
- Lack of empathy

- Interpersonal manipulation
- A calculating view toward others
- Cold-hearted tendencies
- Deceitful

The Machiavellian personality is one that is very cold and negative. This type of person is someone you likely will not get along with from the start of your connection. Because they are so clouded by negativity, they lack awareness of others and situations around them. A Machiavellian individual will not consider that their actions impact more than just themselves. They will act in ways that they know are wrong and hurtful without feeling bad about it.

Similar to narcissists, Machiavellians will also seek out opportunities for instant gratification. They can carefully weigh their options to determine if a situation is worth it for the long-term or if they would instead seek out something more beneficial that is short-term. They are opportunistic individuals that only think about their feelings. Without the guidance of any morals or core beliefs, a Machiavellian individual will aim to get ahead and not be stopped.

This personality type is especially drawn to money and wealth. If they can get ahead financially, you can expect them to take any means necessary to do so, and this mainly includes choosing actions that might hurt the people in their lives. They will also control others around them like pawns in their own game of chess. When they can figure out how to work all of the moving parts of their lives, they are able to guide themselves toward the most successful outcome. A Machiavellian individual is generally brilliant because this strategy requires a lot of careful calculation.

Since they are very opportunistic, they understand which situations will impact their status and which will not. For example, doing a kind favor for you in the privacy of your home is not going to gain them any notoriety. They would rather donate to a charitable cause in a public way or complete volunteer work that they know will be recognized by a large group of people. Basically, if nobody will see them do something kind, they would rather not do it. This behavior is an indication that they are acting on all of the wrong reasons for pursuing kindness.

Despite all of these flaws, Machiavellian individuals are very good at reaching their goals. Because they have so much self-interest, they will stop at nothing to achieve the results they are hoping for. When you do not know what is going on beyond the surface, this might seem like a person who is exceptionally gifted and motivated. You might even be inspired by them, which is why there is a chance you will let them into your life. Don't be fooled by their progress— they gained it deceitfully.

How to Deal with One

You need to set boundaries right away. A Machiavellian individual probably won't respect these boundaries, but if they think there aren't any in place, they will think they have free reign to control you. Once you set these boundaries, you must be firm with them. Always bring them up if they are crossed, and tell the individual why the action is not okay with you. They will make it hard to stick to your boundaries, but this is one of the most important steps you can take to protect yourself.

Accept the reality that this is who they are as a person. The Machiavellian type is notoriously difficult to deal with, and you might feel like it is up to you to fix them if you are close to them—this is never going to work. They need professional care to get to the root of their transgressions. You are going to exhaust yourself if you put too much effort into "fixing" an individual who is like this. The sooner you can come to the reality of acceptance, the sooner you will be able to move on with your life and steer clear of them.

When you interact with a Machiavellian individual, it is important to become aware of your vulnerabilities before they pick up on them. If you know that certain topics bring out your sensitive side, avoid engaging in them with this person. They will use the conversation against you in an attempt for more personal gain. Knowing what makes you upset or what impacts you, they will use it against you every chance they get. This outcome is why keeping these parts of yourself private when you interact with the individual is helpful. They won't be able to know how to read you, and this is exactly what you want.

Build supportive relationships outside of this person. If they mean almost everything to you, they have the potential to disappoint you and devastate you in a big way. Once they show you their true colors and how they are willing to use them against you, it will hurt. You need to make sure that you have a great support system around you that can pick you up if this person puts you down. There are times when being around them is going to be inevitable, but you can still make the most of the situation by protecting yourself.

If you have to be around them often, stick to the basics. Remind yourself that you do not need to engage with them on a deeper level because they do not care to get to know you or to treat you with respect—they are only trying to get close to you to see what this can do for them. Many Machiavellian individuals will stop putting on a front once they realize you can see right through it. It might catch them off guard, but you do not have to be concerned with sparing their feelings. They had the intention to deceive you and use you, so what you do in response is your way of protecting yourself from this.

Psychopath

The main characteristics:

- High impulsivity
- Thrill-seeking behavior
- Low empathy
- Lack of loyalty
- Irresponsibility

A person who is a psychopath will be attracted to situations that put them in a position of power. They will seek out these opportunities in every area of their life. This includes romantic relationships and professional relationships. Even while interacting with their friends and family, a psychopath will seek out moments that they can take that will make them appear powerful. They love to control others, which will lead them to focus on short-term benefits that provide instant gratification—a trait that the above personality types share. Psychopaths are not connected with the consequences of their actions. While they might be aware of precisely what they are doing and how it will impact the environment and others around them, this will not deter them from continuing with their harmful behavior. If you give in to their desires, they will treat you very well. This conduct can be a confusing element of their personality because it gives you a reason to justify their wrongdoings. You might accept them for a very long time before you realize that they are only hurting you. They can be very charismatic and interesting people. Because they love to choose thrill-seeking activities and make impulsive decisions, you might end up becoming captivated by them. This is human nature, and you cannot blame yourself for being interested in a person who appears uninhabited by limitations. You can easily fall in love with a psychopath or desire to be close to them. One big part of the psychopath personality is that they seem to deny many social and societal norms. If they can be different or find certain ways to set themselves apart, they will go for them.

The moment that they hurt you and you realize they do not feel bad about it can be very shocking. If you are under the impression that they care for you and you see their true colors, this is going to be jarring. You have likely put your trust in them already, and before you know it, they have transformed into their true self before your eyes. This type of deception is especially concerning because you have probably already formed a specific conclusion about them in your mind. To know that you shattered this illusion will make you see them very differently. You can think about this as a blessing in disguise.

They will be quick to turn a blind eye to the severity of their actions. Instead of taking accountability for what they have done, they are quick to deny that anything is wrong or to share the blame with those around them. They will likely feel very offended if you call them out for their behavior and suggest that they are not to blame. There are so many negative traits lurking below the surface, and it doesn't take much for them to feel that they can fully express them.

How to Deal with One

You need to have a strong grasp on your emotions when you are dealing with a psychopath. They will try to invalidate you at every chance you get, so the risk of being emotionally manipulated is very high. By standing firm in your beliefs and being true to yourself, you can validate your feelings without completely giving in to the psychopath you are dealing with. This might feel frustrating and upsetting to you, but it is going to make you a lot stronger and better able to handle these types of personalities.

Do your best never to show them that you are intimidated by them, even if you feel this strongly. Psychopaths want you to give up your control to them because they want to overpower them. If you ever try to express that you are a victim of their antics, they will usually turn the situation against you and paint themselves as the victim instead. For example, they might bring up a tragic backstory they have experienced to make you feel sorry for them. It takes the attention away from your feelings and places them in the center of attention again.

A psychopath is going to have a bigger chance of controlling you if you are interacting in person. They will be able to pick up on your energy and read your body language. If you can help it, only interact with them online or over the phone. By placing yourself at a distance, they are not going to feel as satisfied with their need to control you. It isn't impossible for them to still charm you with their ways, even digitally, so be careful with what you say and how much you allow them to get to know you.

Do your best to build up your mental strength. You will need this to handle any regular communication or interaction you must have with a psychopath. Their main goal is to break you down, even despite their kind or exciting exterior. If you are still struggling, you need to try to stay away from them. Any instance of weakness will be spotted right away—this is what psychopaths are best at. They will pinpoint these vulnerabilities in you if you make them easily accessible.

If you are struggling to determine if someone is a psychopath or not, you need to pay attention to their actions and not their words. A deceitful person will typically be great at knowing what to say to get you to trust them, but their actions are still going to appear questionable. If you are able to look at the bigger picture, you will see that they aren't all they say they are. Your heightened senses allow you to have the upper hand and protect yourself from their attempts to control you.

Conclusion

You now have a lot of insightful information that you can use while dealing with people who might not have your best intentions in mind. The world can be a scary place full of individuals who want to take advantage of you, but you no longer have to live in fear. You have the tools necessary to protect yourself and to distance yourself from all of the manipulators, abusers, and toxic people in your life. By building up your strength, you will see newfound personal growth throughout this process.

Mind control is potent, but it is futile against a mind that knows what it wants and what it stands for. Give yourself credit for staying true to who you are, as this is what a manipulative person will try to exploit. You are strong enough to handle anything and anyone that comes your way, regardless of how dark or toxic they are. If you are currently in a bad situation with a manipulative individual, you can now make a plan of action using your resources.

Be cautious of who you let into your life because not everyone has the same intentions as you do. Once you realize just how far manipulators are willing to deceive you, this will give you an entirely new perspective. It is going to allow you to move past the need for any further interaction with bad people, and it will show you how to focus on the great things and connections that you have in your life. You do not deserve to be treated with anything less than someone's full respect. Use this as your power and your mantra. As you try to work through the intentions of those in your life, you can always feel confident in your ability to avoid dark psychology and manipulation.

References

Beohm, R. (2020, February 6). *What To Do When You See "Negative" Body Language.* Rachel Beohm | Writer, Speaker, Coach. https://www.rachelbeohm.com/what-to-do-when-you-see-negative-body-language/.

Garnett, L. (2016, March 3). *How to Know If You Are Brainwashed, and What to Do to Avoid It.* Inc.com. https://www.inc.com/laura-garnett/how-to-know-if-you-are-brainwashed-and-what-to-do-to-avoid-it.html.

Harmer, S. (2018, May 2). *8 Ways To Stop Emotional Manipulation.* Lifehack. https://www.lifehack.org/articles/lifestyle/8-ways-stop-emotional-manipulation.html.

Holland, K. (2018, February 13). *15+ Signs of Emotion Manipulation.* Healthline. https://www.healthline.com/health/mental-health/emotional-manipulation.

Lamar, C. (2015, December 16). *10 mind control clichés (and how to avoid them).* io9. https://io9.gizmodo.com/10-mind-control-cliches-and-how-to-avoid-them-5836169.

Louv, J. (2017, May 10). *10 Ways to Protect Yourself From NLP Mind Control.* Ultraculture. https://ultraculture.org/blog/2014/01/16/nlp-10-ways-protect-mind-control/.

Nuccitelli, M. (2020, August 15). *#DarkPsychology - Dark Side of #HumanConsciousness Concept.* iPredator. https://www.ipredator.co/dark-psychology/.

Raychev, M. (2014, July 29). *10 Tips That Will Help You Avoid Emotional Manipulation.* I Heart Intelligence.com. https://iheartintelligence.com/avoid-manipulation/.

Sussex Publishers. Deception. Psychology Today. https://www.psychologytoday.com/us/basics/decepti

on.

The Mind Tools Content Team. *Body Language: Picking Up and Understanding Nonverbal Signals.* https://www.mindtools.com/pages/article/Body_Language.htm.

University of Copenhagen. (2018, September 26). *Psychologists define the 'dark core of personality'.* ScienceDaily. https://www.sciencedaily.com/releases/2018/09/180926110841.htm.

Wu, W., Wang, H., Lee, H., Lin, Y., & Guo, F. (2019, March 21). *How Machiavellianism, Psychopathy, and Narcissism Affect Sustainable Entrepreneurial Orientation: The Moderating Effect of Psychological Resilience.* Frontiers. https://www.frontiersin.org/articles/10.3389/fpsyg.2019.00779/full.

Young, K. (2020, August 13). *15 Signs of a Toxic Relationship.* Hey Sigmund. https://www.heysigmund.com/toxic-relationship-15-signs/.

Printed in Great Britain
by Amazon